Sacred Paths

A Journey Through the Big Questions

Sacred Paths

A Journey Through the Big Questions

Editor

Adrian Gibb BA MA

CHRISTIAN
ALTERNATIVE

Winchester, UK
Washington, USA

First published by Christian Alternative Books, 2013
Christian Alternative Books is an imprint of John Hunt Publishing Ltd.,
Laurel House, Station Approach,
Alresford, Hants, SO24 9JH, UK
office1@jhpbooks.net
www.johnhuntpublishing.com
www.christian-alternative.com

For distributor details and how to order please visit the 'Ordering' section on our website.

Text copyright: Adrian Gibb 2013

ISBN: 978 1 78279 096 9

A CIP catalogue record for this book is available from the British Library.

Design: Stuart Davies

Printed in the USA by Edwards Brothers Malloy

We operate a distinctive and ethical publishing philosophy in all areas of our business, from our global network of authors to production and worldwide distribution.

CONTENTS

Prayer of Saint Francis of Assissi

"Lord, make me an instrument of your peace: where there is hatred, let me sow love: where there is injury, pardon; where there is doubt, faith; where there is despair, hope; where there is darkness, light; and where there is sadness, joy."
Saint Francis of Assisi

For Mary-Jane and Hamish,
Ailig and Ebi

Acknowledgements

I would like to thank, with all my heart, those who gave their time and efforts in contributing to this book. Some were friends before this project started, some I met as a part of this journey, but all I admire greatly and all will, hopefully, consider themselves a part of a unique fellowship.

As always I thank my family and friends who make life so joyful, and my wife and my boy, my sun and my son, the makers of my happiness, and the reason for everything!

Adrian Gibb
Editor – Sacred Paths

Foreword

I remember as a child being told that the only true and living God was the god of Christianity.

Both my mother and grandmother made this assertion with supreme enthusiasm. As a youngster I didn't question much of what they taught and insisted that I learned. My upbringing was that of a young black boy in South Florida who was raised as a devout Primitive Baptist. In my early youth God was real, a living being who lived just beyond the clouds. 'He', as always believed to be, was caring and loving. Yet 'He' possessed a sort of 'Mr. Hyde' personality that lived just beneath 'His' holy skin. It was believed that when you disobeyed your parents or the law of the Church, that God would rise up and create a universal darkness in your life that would plague you until you repented and corrected the wrong. Well, those days are no more.

As I grew older and ventured off into the wild world of education and travel, I learned that many of the teachings and information that I had been brought up to believe weren't empirical or correct. I've studied religion most of my life. I've pastored in Christian churches, and even eaten among the monks of both Theravada and Shin Buddhism. You see, when I ventured from home, I came to know that the greatest part of my growth would come through having insight and information about faith from others' religious cultures. Today, I am a long way religiously from where I came. I am a Buddhist monk who leads an Interfaith Temple congregation and a Buddhist center in the Bible belt of rural North Carolina. I learned to cultivate a spirit of mutual respect and interactive/engaged faith as a result of the experience of coming together and listening. As a monk I practice what is called Daishin Buddhism, or 'big mind' Buddhism. By 'big mind', I mean emptiness of mind or idea, or perception. Open to all things and all beings. My contact with and tutelage of many great religious figures in my life taught me the value and worth of co-engaging in a manner that aids all sentient beings. Even my upbringing, and the teachings of my parents, has contributed to my journey.

If 'Insight and Information' were elements within the Periodic Table, then this book would rank among one of the greatest elements you'll have the honor to explore. As the Periodic Table itself was compiled after years of research and exploration of the foundational elements of our planet, biology, and chemistry, so is this work. Adrian Gibb offers the elements of diversity, perspective, and spiritual congruence on one of the most widely regarded subjects in the Universe: Religion. It offers the testimony of living, breathing, dynamic people from a variety of religious cultures who tell of their spiritual journeys. It also holds a wealth of beautiful and insightful dialogue from Mr. Gibb himself in a manner that only he, as an interfaith facilitator, can do. His ability to capture and articulate the essence of interfaith and religious diversity is splendid, indeed.

Read joyously, with a big mind and a big smile, and be filled with everything.

Namaste.
Bushi Yamato Damashii/Dr. T. Marquis Ramsey
St. Stephen Interfaith Temple & Daishin Buddhist Center
Thomasville, North Carolina

Introduction

This book has had its genesis over many years of searching.

Searching for my own faith, yes, but also searching for that which binds, and acknowledging and respecting that which does not. It is a book packed to the parameters with the knowledge of people I admire greatly, people who are at the coal face of their faiths. As I began writing to those I hoped would contribute, I did not seek academics, though some of the contributors have an academic background. I did not seek theologians, nor necessarily 'leaders' of respective faith traditions, though some of the contributors do indeed serve in that capacity for their own community. What I did seek, forcefully and thoughtfully, were people who lived their faith. People who, on a daily basis, found their day brighter, their sounds sweeter, because of the conscious choice they have made to believe in a particular path. It is a group of individuals, and it is important to note that; a reflection from a particular member of a faith does not mean all in that faith feel that way. Indeed, this is a central part of the goal of this book.

In asking members of various faiths, from various locations around the world, five 'big questions', this book hopes to promote a pluralistic attitude towards many faiths, examine how each person responds as a representative of the 'label' they feel comfortable with, but also to show, within that, that there are differing attitudes within each faith. This is an important and often misunderstood point within pluralistic and interfaith dialogue. A Mahayana Buddhist will have a different take to a Theravada Buddhist. A Hellenic Pagan will have a different take to a Celtic one. Within each faith tradition, many views may be held. There is, you may say, pluralism within each faith itself. In reading this book, hopefully, you will see these differences in some of these faiths.

I have been involved in interfaith and multifaith work for many years now. I have organised fellowship dinners between Pagans and Christians, talks from Bahai authors, Buddhists, representatives from Orthodox Judaism, the Liberal Catholic Church, even, on one fascinating and memorable evening, a Scientologist. These evenings and meetings have been fundamentally 'good'. They have increased the knowledge of, and understanding of, a myriad of different faiths and belief systems, for me, and for the many others who have joined me on this journey. What have I learned through this journey? In November of 2010 I was asked to speak to a group of students doing a course entitled 'A Theology of Religious Pluralism' at Trinity Theological College here in Brisbane. I was asked to reflect on what I had learned through my interfaith work to that date. I came up with four major points:

Mystery: Many reading this book will be familiar with the Four Blind Men and the Elephant Story. If you haven't, the analogy is as follows. Four blind men find something blocking their path. They each reach out to discover what it is. The first feels what he says is like a palm tree, the second says it is a substantial wall. A third states it is nothing more than a piece of rope. And the fourth blind man says he can feel the flapping wing of a bird. In turn, each had touched a different part of an elephant, the first the trunk, the second the body, the third the tail and the fourth an ear. Each of them is touching a separate part of the elephant, and, due to their not being able to see, it is this, and only this, that can inform their ideas about what is in front of them. They are dealing with the mystery as best they can, with their own experiences to guide them. Over the years I have found this story very useful, and also, very true. By accepting and embracing the concept that, ultimately, we can't 'nail down' or limit, or 'know', with absolute certainty, what the Divine is, we can then make a fundamental and important step. We can begin to ask, 'Okay, we

4

are like the blind men, this is what I am feeling, what my experience tells me of the Divine, what are you feeling, what are you experiencing?' This step leads to dialogue, understanding and, above all, respect for difference!

Vive le Difference: A common mistake in interfaith work, in my opinion, is a misguided attempt, with the best of intentions, to foster fellowship and dialogue with other faiths by abandoning key aspects of your own faith, which you may feel will 'offend' those of different traditions. But it is important to embrace the differences rather than seek the lowest common denominator. Don't abandon key aspects on faith just to foster dialogue. Marcus Borg, when relating a story of the Dalai Lama telling a Christian to not become a Buddhist, but become as good a Christian as she can be, said this:

> "By living more deeply into our own tradition as a sacrament of the sacred, we become more centered in the one to whom the tradition points and in whom we live and move and have our being.
>
> A Christian is one who does this within the framework of the Christian tradition, just as a Jew is one who does this within the framework of the Jewish tradition, a Muslim, within the framework of the Muslim tradition, and so forth. And I cannot believe that God cares which of these we are. All are paths of relationship and transformation." [1]

Whether you agree with Borg as to whether God cares about these frameworks, it is important to acknowledge that there are differences, sometimes great differences, between the faiths. There are also, exquisitely, incredible similarities, ones that we can hold on to, and learn by, and increase in our own faith by. But we do this by addressing those ties that bind, and those that don't. Acknowledging all, respecting all, and moving on from there.

Horses for courses: It is important to note that different religions want to do different things. A Theravada Buddhist will approach her/his path, the way she/he meditates, the goals and aspirations of Buddhism in a different way to a Mahayana Buddhist. One may reject all that is metaphysical, the other see this as vital to their faith. Personality traits can even determine a person's faith or journey within a faith. One person may be contemplative and mystical, another interested in ritual and intellectual discourse, while another may see their faith as bound within social action and good deeds. If a person is fascinated by what comes after we die, that will determine their faith journey, or perhaps complement it, while others, for instance many Jewish people, see their faith as firmly couched in the life we are living, and that takes precedence over more eschatological issues. One of the participants in one of my interfaith groups posited the notion that personality tests should be done to determine which faith would suit you more. I think there is something in that notion. Obviously the point is that the variety of faiths and belief systems allow these differences within goals and/or 'personalities' to be satisfied. The difference, the diversity, fosters a continuation of faith as a whole, and does not destroy it.

Inter-Culture as much as Interfaith: I have found that it is not so much different faiths, per se, that needs to get on, but different cultures. Cultural manipulation of scripture is the main source for conflict. I have spoken to Muslim Imams who can recite chapter and verse on how the Koran insists on peace, love, and respect for other faiths and other people. Needless to say others of that faith, spurred on by their surroundings, their geo-political situations, their poverty even, may focus on other aspects of that sacred text. A progressive Celtic Christian raised in Australia, like me, is going to have a completely different Christianity to an Ethiopian Coptic Christian, though we worship the same reflection of the Divine and read from the same scriptures. This is because the cultures we have been raised in are completely different. Faith is changed, moulded by, the culture in which that faith resides. But this is, or at least can be, a very positive notion to embrace. It means that, before we deal with complex faith questions, we need to, at a human level, respect the person, appreciate and understand their cultural background and then respect and discuss the faith of that person within that environment.

All of the above has informed not only this book but all interfaith and multifaith dialogue I engage in. After this introduction you will see short biographies of those who have contributed to this book. After that is a section called 'Avatars'. I asked each contributor to supply me with a symbol, or an image, that, for them, summed up their faith, and their relationship with that faith. An explanation will appear with each Avatar. Then, in the substantive chapters, it will be the Avatar that introduces a contribution to the chapter, rather than a name. In doing this I hope to take away some pre-conceptions. Rather than a name or a label, an image will move us into the words, often stunningly beautiful images, images that mean a great deal to the contributors. Another hope is that, as you, the reader, progress through this book, you take note of the images that you find yourself searching for, or perhaps the images that make you take notice when you see them. Perhaps a deeper respect for a particular faith, if not all the faiths contained in this work, can be found. It should be noted, as will be obvious, that not every single faith is represented in this book. While it was impossible to find contributors from all of the diverse panorama of faiths and belief systems throughout the world (and it wasn't from the lack of trying), the contributors in this book represent a broad spectrum of faiths, some often terribly under-represented or even misrepresented in the media, and, as mentioned above, branches within these faiths. These contributors have been chosen also because they share with me a similar outlook as to the importance of interfaith dialogue and education.

Despite what some would have us believe, faith can be a force for the most positive transformation and compassion, a bridge, via the limitless divine, between people, cultures and beliefs. This book aims to shine a light on the exquisite aspects of faith, the beauty of those willing to give up their time and energy to foster faith, and finally to the ongoing and noble goal that is interfaith dialogue.

Adrian Gibb BA MA
Brisbane, Australia 2013

SACRED PATHS CONTRIBUTORS

Susan Handley – Bahá'í

I am a first generation Bahá'í. I was raised in a small rural town in Massachusetts, United States of America, as a member of the Congregationalist Church (the United Church of Christ) which encouraged enquiry into the nature of humanity and how best to serve it in the spirit of the love of Christ. I then went to Harvard University and was exposed to a great diversity of philosophies and challenged to define my own understanding of the nature of reality. In my search for truth I travelled to many different countries around the world and visited the holy places of many different faiths. I found kindred spirits sincerely searching for truth in every place and every faith – it was clear that the spiritual qualities such as love, kindness, and generosity were present in people in every land, irrespective of race, religion, nationality, gender or class.

At home and in my travels I met Bahá'ís and learned that in the nineteenth century Bahá'u'lláh, the prophet founder of the Bahá'í Faith, specifically taught of the oneness of humanity and outlined principles (such as equality of women and men, abolition of prejudice, harmony between science and religion and elimination of extremes in poverty and wealth) to guide humanity to maturity and peace. These principles also include universal education and independent investigation of truth. In the Bahá'í Faith there are no clergy. When questions arise we are advised to consult with learned believers and elected institutions. Community affairs are run by annually elected Assemblies, on which any adult believer can be called to serve.

In November 1989, after two years of prayerfully studying the Bahá'í writings and attending a number of its community activities, I knew that I believed in the teachings of Bahá'u'lláh and declared as a Bahá'í. Since that time I have been an active member of Bahá'í communities in several countries (including Austria, the USA and Australia) and have served in various capacities including on elected assemblies, appointed task forces and as a teacher of children's classes. I have also had the privilege of spending nine years as an executive aide/researcher/analyst/writer at the international centre of the Bahá'í Faith in Haifa, Israel.

One of the principles of the Bahá'í Faith is that work is worship, when carried out in a spirit of service to humanity. Before serving in Haifa I had obtained a Masters degree in teaching science to grades 5-12 and spent four years as a teacher. After completing my service in Haifa, my Australian husband and I moved to Brisbane, where I have since worked as a legal secretary and as an executive assistant for Indigenous Partnerships in the Queensland Department of Education and Training. I have also served as a representative of the Queensland Branch of the Australian Bahá'í Community and have organised and participated in a number of interfaith activities to promote multicultural understanding and peace.

Raymond Lam – Mahayana Buddhist

I am the editor of Buddhistdoor International, a non-profit website owned by Tung Lin Kok Yuen, a Hong Kong and Vancouver-based Buddhist charity. The responses in this book are Raymond Lam's personal opinions and do not reflect his editorial position on Buddhistdoor.com or for Tung Lin Kok Yuen. My academic interest in ecumenical theology may be related to my passion about the history of Central Asia and the Silk Routes, where a staggering diversity of cultures, economies, religions and empires converged and met. I converted to Mahāyāna Buddhism in 2008 after spending my teen years reading about world religions. I belong to the Chinese Buddhist tradition, but it has always been hard for me to maintain any real sectarian boundaries between different Buddhist traditions. I like to believe that I'm an ecumenist, for the Buddha taught that the potentiality of spiritual perfection dwells in every creature. It is never lost, only obscured. Since Buddhism posits rebirth, this potentiality can always be unveiled once more.

Rev. Mark Townsend – Progressive Christian

A former clergyman in the Church of England, Reverend Mark Townsend now leads his own inclusive and ecumenical ministry that nourishes a strong appreciation for the diversity of faith beyond Christianity, and which strives to honor the divine in all people, regardless of their faith, culture, sexuality or background.

A priest of the Open Episcopal Church and member of the Progressive Christian Alliance, in addition to being a member of the Order of Bards, Ovates and Druids, the author has been featured on the BBC and several other news programs throughout Britain. He is the author of *The Gospel of Falling Down*, and *Jesus Outside the Box* (O Books). He lives in Hereford, England.

Rabbi Shoshanna Kaminsky – Judaism

I grew up just outside of Washington, DC as part of a substantial Jewish community. There were approximately 200,000 Jews living in the DC-metropolitan area when I was a child, which is about twice the total Jewish population of Australia! I never remarked on it, but a substantial percentage of my public school class—perhaps 15% were Jewish. A whopping 33% of my university classmates were Jewish as well, although many of them were actively rebelling against their faith at the time.

I was raised in a Reform Jewish household in which tradition was important but faith was generally not discussed. In the classical Reform approach that I learned primarily from my mother, human beings acted ethically because that was what God expected of us. There was little hope of a reward or even any close connection with God, who I learned was quite remote. When I began my seminary studies, I realised that the approach I had been raised with fit solidly into the philosophy of the medieval rabbi and theologian Rabbi Moses ben Maimon, popularly known as Maimonides. Maimonides taught that God was so utterly removed from humanity that we could never hope for any kind of meaningful relationship with God. The best he could imagine would be us comprehending just a bit of the divine nature.

My spirituality and sense of faith was transformed through a number of significant encounters. The first was when I joined up with a group of women Jewish seekers in university. In our small circle, we explored Jewish women's spirituality, which in the mid-1980s was just beginning to find its voice. A further dramatic encounter was my first experience of meeting theological students from the Christian tradition, who spoke powerfully of their personal relationship with God. Through them, I began to imagine that I too could actually connect with God. Finally, I experienced my faith through the two years I spent working as a hospital chaplain following my ordination in 1994. I found God in the hospital room and particularly in those liminal moments that occur in times of crisis.

For the last fifteen years, I have led a more mundane existence as a congregational rabbi. I served a small community outside of Pittsburgh for ten years, and for the last five, I have served an equally small community in Adelaide, South Australia. My spiritual life has been enhanced greatly by my two sons Yonatan and Nadav who are my greatest gifts from God.

Janine Evans – Muslim

I grew up in Adelaide after migrating from England with my family when I was 2 years old. I studied design and travelled the world living and working in many countries before returning to Adelaide in 1992. It was around this time that I also 'embraced Islam' and married. My South African husband and I have 3 sons who are as 'Aussie' as they are Muslim. The events of 9/11 changed my life forever and I have worked extensively to break down media stereotypes around the 'Australian Muslim' community. In 2007 I published my first book '2 veil or not 2 veil – the life of an Aussie Muslim' which describes my journey from mainstream Christian Australian to minority Muslim Australian and how the current world political climate affects my family and community on a daily basis, especially the misconceptions we have in the west around Islam.

In the decade that followed the bombing of the Twin Towers, I pursued the area of cross cultural/religious training which has often given me the opportunity to develop strategies for looking at life through someone else's eyes. My conversion has given me first-hand experience of having to negotiate my way around a new way of life and the many new cultures that exist in the

Australian Muslim community, I often have the opportunity to build bridges between the culture I call my own (Anglo-Saxon Australian) and the 70 different ethnic groups that exist within the Australian Muslim community.

Elizabeth McNally – Wiccan

Elizabeth first stepped out upon her path more than a quarter of a century ago in Religious Studies at the University of Ottawa, Canada where she was first introduced to Paganism and Witchcraft. She studied as a Solitaire practitioner for a decade before eventually finding her way to her now long time friend, mentor and High Priestess, Lady Wren. Under Wren's tutelage Elizabeth elevated to High Priestess in The Newly Revised Circle of the Mystic Grove on Imbolc, 2008 in Northern California. In a Passing of the Wand ritual at Alban Eiler, 2008, Elizabeth became the High Priestess of the Newly Revised Circle of the Mystic Grove. She moved to the DC area in that same year. In DC, she was fortunate to find herself in community with Iris Firemoon and Circle of the Spiral Moon, where she initiated under Iris and spent a period of study in pursuit of further knowledge in the area of Clergy and Interfaith work, before returning to her native Canada in 2010. Through a series of synchronous happenings it became clear that her path at her current crossroads was to be interfaith work. Elizabeth was introduced to Father Mark Townsend, a Vicar, Magician, and Druid residing in England and together they conceived the idea of an online Church for those looking to build bridges between faiths. Hedge-Church was established on Facebook, with Father Townsend at the Helm, Peter Owen-Jones of BBC's Around the World in 80 Faiths, as Patron, administrators of differing faiths residing in continents around the world, and members of widely varying faiths and beliefs throughout the world.

Ajmer Gill – Sikh

Ajmer Singh Gill is the President of the Sikh Council of Australia, the umbrella body of the Sikh community in Australia. He was born in Singapore, raised in Malaysia and studied in England. He worked in Malaysia before coming to Australia in 1981 and working as an educator in such diverse places as Western Australia, Northern Territory and New South Wales. He served as Senior Education Officer in Darwin, the capital of Northern Territory, Australia.

Ajmer is passionate about the work of the Sikh Council of Australia and has displayed great leadership in addressing Sikh issues and educating the public about Sikhs. He helps Sikh community members to play a full role in Australian life, and he contributes on their behalf to national and local government policy. In 2004 he organised the first ever Australian World Sikh Conference, and from 2007 onwards he has managed the participation of Sikhs in the annual Sydney ANZAC Day March.

Ajmer recognises that Youth is the Future and has worked hard to organise camps and forums since 1998. In 2005 he received the NSW Community Relations Commission Award for

Community Service.

Under Ajmer's leadership, various community development projects, focussing on Integration, Awareness and Harmony have been successfully delivered, including courses for Sikh Scouts, World Sikh Conference, Multifaith Projects, Sikh Youth Camps and Projects like Domestic Bliss. He has been the driving force behind the development of the NSW Punjabi Language Syllabus to HSC level in NSW.

He is an Executive member of the Ethnic Communities Council of NSW, a member of the Board of Management of the Hills Holroyd Parramatta Migrant Resource Centre and the Boronia Multicultural Centre, and a member of the Sydney Alliance.

Ajmer coordinates Sikh Special Religious Education in NSW besides actively promoting Human Rights Education in the Sikh community. He is a Marriage Celebrant of the Sikh Council of Australia and is responsible for all other Celebrants of the Council in Australia.

Ajmer is a member of the World Council of Religions for Peace (NSW) and presented a paper at the Parliament of World Religions in Melbourne 2009.

Dan Walker – Vodou

Daniel lives in Brisbane, Australia, and was awarded his PhD from the University of Queensland for his thesis entitled "Fixing and Healing: Vodou and Social Change in New Orleans". He spent several months in post-Katrina New Orleans speaking with people about their experiences with Vodou, either first-hand or as an observer. Daniel worked particularly with the Vodou House of *La Source Ancienne Ounfo*, led by Manbo Sallie Ann Glassman, whose healing-based approach to this religion is shaping the growth of Vodou in New Orleans. Daniel's research interests continue to be Vodou and other Afro-Caribbean religions, as well as other experiential and particularly magic-based traditions. He currently works at the University of Queensland.

Gede Parma – Pagan

Gede Parma Akheron is a Wild Witch, Pagan Mystic, initiated Priest and award-winning author. His published works to date are *Spirited: Taking Paganism Beyond the Circle, By Land, Sky & Sea* and *Ecstatic Witchcraft*. He is an initiate and teacher of the WildWood Tradition of Witchcraft; a hereditary healer and seer with Balinese-Celtic ancestry. He is the lover of and devoted to nine gorgeous and ever-deep Potencies – Persephone, Aphrodite, Hekate, Hermes, the Blue God, the Weaver, the Green Man, the Crescent-Crowned Goddess and the Horned-Cloaked God. He is an Anderson Feri student, a Reclaiming Witch and also studies in the Anderean Current of Old Craft. He is a vessel, a diviner, a spell-caster and spirit-worker who adores the Mysterious Craft.

Gede has devoted his life to communities striving for 'excellence and elegance', and that in Love, Truth and Wisdom commit to walking through the Gates of Paradise and opening to Beauty. He likes to laugh, play, cry, eat, dance, sing, wyrd-out, pray and make ceremony with other Cunning Folk and Bright Spirits and is earnest in his love of 'dreaming big' and daring to enact those dreams for our Holy-Whole Cosmos. Gede is a poet and priestess of the Black, Wild Heart and endlessly hopes to help others realise the Divine. Gede has an Erotic Relationship with God and would love to see more of this in the World.

Adrian Gibb – Celtic Christian

Adrian was born in East London, South Africa, his family emigrating to Australia in 1978 and settling in Brisbane.

In 2004 Adrian completed a Masters degree in Studies in Religion and is currently a PhD student within the school of History, Philosophy, Religion and Classics at the University of Queensland. Founder and co-coordinator of PAX (Progressive Anglican Christians) and one of the original admins for the online multifaith community Hedge-Church, Adrian is a passionate advocate for interfaith dialogue and pluralistic fellowship.

Adrian has been published widely in various publications in the form of short stories, articles and novels and is the creator and editor of Sacred Paths.

Alastair Gornall – Theravada Buddhist

Theravada Buddhism largely encompasses the beliefs and practices of Buddhists in Sri Lanka and much of continental Southeast Asia. Alastair Gornall has been a practising Theravada Buddhist for nearly 10 years. He is currently completing a PhD in South Asian Studies at the University of Cambridge and was President of the University of London Buddhist Association in 2009. His scholarly and writing interests are broad, encompassing Buddhist history, anthropology, travels in Asia and modern questions about the spiritual life.

Linda Ward – Celtic Pagan

Linda has been a practicing Pagan for over forty-five years, working mainly as a solitary and following the Celtic traditions. She is an active member of the Pagan community in south-east Queensland. She has a graduate diploma in Religious Studies from Queensland University (2003) and is a graduate of Griffith University's MultiFaith Centre In-Service Development Training Program in Interfaith Dialogue and Understanding (2009). In December 2009 Linda was honoured to be part of the panel, Australian Pagans Speak, at the Parliament of the World's Religions in Melbourne. In 2010 she contributed to the book *Spirituality, Conversations and Community-Building*, a joint project of AMARAH and Misbah. During 2011 Linda presented on Paganism and Pagan beliefs to Believing Women for a Culture of Peace and at several events at the MultiFaith Centre at Griffith University. She was one of the faith representatives speaking to the importance of the Declaration of Human Rights at Amnesty International's 50th birthday. In early 2012 Linda presented at the first of a series of Multifaith forums on the topic "Who is My God?" organised by the Queensland Jewish Community Services Inc and the Roman Catholic Commission for Ecumenism and Inter-Religious Relations. This presentation led to requests from both WomenSpace and the Brisbane Theosophical Society to speak on her understanding of Celtic Pagan deity.

Avatars

Raymond Lam – Mahayana Buddhist

The Dharma Wheel represents the Buddha's Eightfold Path with its eight spokes. I chose this avatar because it is one of the traditional solar symbols of early Buddhism, along with the footprint, the tree, and the empty throne. It resonates with me because it imparts teachings to humanity without being anthropomorphic, embodies the essence of the Buddha's path, and offers wholeness and tranquillity to any who meditate and reflect on its Dharmic nature. It embodies Dharma, which is not only the right way to live but also reality itself. That is a Buddhist's hope: to live correctly, grounded in reality.

Gede Parma – Pagan

In the Anderson Feri/Faery Tradition of Witchcraft the Peacock Angel Melek Taus, revered and beloved especially by the Yezidi people of modern-day Iraq, is one of the personages of the Blue God. The Blue God embodies the collective consciousness of humanity and our own innate capacity to become whole beings of power, mystery, truth, wisdom and love. In many ways the

Blue God bears striking similarities to the Christ and Krishna and indeed Krishna is portrayed as a blue-skinned god and bears the plumage of peacocks. In the WildWood Tradition of Witchcraft we sometimes draw and enliven the 'Peacock Eye'—Calling out to the Wild Feast, we draw in the Green Fire of the Wild. This fire is the Current of the Greening and represents Nature's endurance, strength and timeless spirit—She will ever rise! This is the Fire that opens the door through the Blue Fire of Faerie, of Infinite Creativity, to the Wild Heart of our original innocence, original blessing—we recall Paradise and we claim it with the Sovereignty of Self that is bestowed upon us by the Grace of God Herself. We re-member our Divinity and deepen into our limitlessness; we enjoin ourselves to the Infinite All. The Peacock Eye is a symbol of this Great Work—the Work that I have committed to serve and celebrate in fullness, here and now.

Dan Walker – Vodou

This symbol is the Veve of Papa Legba, a very old and significant *lwa* of Vodou. He is summoned in each ceremony, as the keeper of the crossroads between the physical and spiritual worlds. His veve is drawn upon the ground, acting as a beacon or marker for Legba to enter and allow the ceremony to continue. Each *lwa* or family of *lwa* has its own veve—some are very simple, and others are extremely ornate and beautiful. They each relate to the *lwa* in some way. Legba's veve features a cross, symbolising the crossroad, and on one side shows a straight stick which represents Legba's walking cane. When summoned, Legba appears as an old man, bent at the waist and walking with the aid of a cane.

Janine Evans – Muslim

The avatar I have chosen is the Crescent Moon—it is the symbol that represents Islam and is often seen accompanied by a five pointed star which represents the Five Pillars of Islam: Belief in one God, Prayer, Fasting, Charity and Pilgrimage.

As Muslims we are taught that we are constantly on a journey and it is our responsibility to grow and learn in many ways— emotionally, spiritually, socially and intellectually. The Prophet Mohammed (peace be upon him) said 'seek knowledge from the cradle to the grave'. Like the crescent moon we are not complete but always searching and learning with room to grow and be filled with the wonders that surround us everyday.

When I learned the reason this symbol represents Islam I was deeply moved and I am honoured to be connected to it in some small way.

Susan Handley – Bahá'í

The symbol I have chosen is an artistic rendition of a nine

pointed star. In the Arabic language (in which many of the original Bahá'í writings are revealed), each letter has a numerical value. The letters in the word "Bahá" add up to the number nine, a symbol of unity. Unity is a key.principle in the Bahá'í teachings. Bahá'ís believe that there is one God, that there is a fundamental truth uniting the great world religions, and that humanity is one family which will unite to form one global civilization.

"Bahá" means glory, splendour or light. "Bahá" is also a title by which Bahá'u'lláh (1817-92), the Prophet-Founder of the Bahá'í Faith is sometimes designated. The full translation of Bahá'u'lláh is "The Glory of God".

Bahá'í means follower of glory, or follower of Bahá'u'lláh.

Linda Ward – Celtic Pagan

The earliest archaeological evidence of the triple spiral dates back to 3200 BCE where it is found carved into the entrance stone at Newgrange in Ireland, as well as in the inner chamber that is illuminated by the equinox sunrise. Its symbolism is multi-layered and is based on the sacred nature of the number three in Celtic traditions. It can be seen to represent the Triple Goddess aspects of Maiden, Mother and Crone; the life phases of Life, Death and Rebirth; the moon phases of waxing, full and waning; the realms of Land, Sea and Sky; the three life elements of Body, Mind and Spirit; and the three time elements of Past, Present and Future.

Rabbi Shoshanna Kaminsky – Judaism

The image I have chosen is a lion. Specifically, this lion is pictured in one of the stained glass windows created by Andrew Steiner for my synagogue Beit Shalom. Although I was born 10,000 miles from Adelaide, Beit Shalom ("house of peace") has come to feel like home, and I associate this lion with that home. I have also chosen the lion, because it is an ancient symbol of the Tribe of Judah and of the Jewish people as a whole. Although I am in no way a believer in astrology, I was born under the sign of Leo, and so I have felt a connection to the lion for much of my life. Finally, the lion is a symbol of quiet strength. In the last three years, I have strayed far beyond my comfort zone and become a student of the martial arts. The lion here represents my efforts to reinvent myself as someone able to defend myself if needed.

Adrian Gibb – Celtic Christian

This is a version of the logo for Hedge-Church, an online inter-faith community that I am a member of and, I am proud to say, was one of the original three admins for. With some 700 members from around the world, from Christians to Muslims and Pagans to Buddhists, it is an exquisite example of how people from disparate faiths and backgrounds can come together in fellowship and even love. For me, the above image, designed by a fellow member, speaks completely of my combined faiths of Christianity and Celtic tradition.

Ajmer Gill – Sikh

Ek Oangkar, consisting of the Punjabi numeral Ek (one) and Oangkar, meaning 'there is one God', 'one reality'.

This is what resonates with me. This is what I believe Sikhi is about. Sikhs believe in one universal God no matter what name is utilised to describe this entity. There is but one God. Sikhs believe in worshipping the One God (Puja Akal Ki) who lives every-where and in the hearts of all. Sikhs believe different religions are different paths to realize God. Sikhi asks a non-Sikh to discover and live the essential message and meaning of his/her own religion so that a Christian can become a better Christian, a Jew a better Jew, a Hindu a better Hindu, while a Sikh becomes a better Sikh.

Elizabeth McNally – Wiccan

The pentacle represents my Pagan earth based Spiritual path and is an eternity symbol with all the elements (earth, air, fire and water) in harmony with Spirit. The cross represents my bridge from my Pagan path back to the teachings of Jesus, whose message I feel is in harmony with my personal path. The key is symbolic of the unlocking of my Spiritual path which continues to evolve, and will until I breathe my last breath in this realm.

Rev. Mark Townsend – Progressive Christian

This avatar is made up of the Christian Cross and the Druid Awen.

The Cross needs no explanation of course, though to me (and many more Progressive Christians) it does not represents a violent sacrifice to an Almighty 'Deity' who demands some sort of transaction in blood, but the consequences of a God-soaked life of courage and personal sacrifice. Jesus, through the Cross, paid the price not to an angry God but to an angry humanity. He ended up there because he challenged human belief systems which kept other humans in their place. It is thus symbolic of costly human/divine love. The Awen /I\ is the modern Druid symbol for inspiration from above (the sun's rays coming down from the sky). I see a deep harmony in connecting these two powerful symbols and using them as one. They also connect my own dual-faith as I myself walk with one foot in each world.

Alastair Gornall – Theravada Buddhist

I have chosen to use the footprints of the Buddha as my avatar. Footprints such as these are often used by Buddhists, especially in Sri Lanka and Thailand, as a symbolic representation of the Buddha. I particularly like this iconic representation of the Buddha since it conveys his presence yet inherent emptiness.

CHAPTER ONE

What is God?

I believe in a limitless divine, within and without, immanent and beyond, past, present, future, out of time, genderless and genderfull, a sacred paradox, supremely love, a creator, a liberator, but also the summerlands and discarnate realm. I have heard many Christians, and people of other faiths for that matter, talk about certainty. It is certainty that is yearned for, a faith based not in metaphor or myth, parable or perception, but real, black and white, here and now, solid certainty! Indeed, I heard a conservative evangelical preacher saying that creation as stated in the Bible should be taken literally for the very simple reason that God wanted our faith to be a real part of our life, not a spiritual explanation for a scientific process, but the reality, the truth, certainty!

Yet, when I think of such certainty, it leaves me cold! Is it just me? If I could know, for certain, exactly what God is, exactly which parts of the Bible must be adhered to and which not, exactly which faith is right and which is wrong, if my faith was reduced to 'following the rules', well, I think I would be bored out of my skull. More importantly, I would be living a faith which, I believe, is spiritually deficient! Why? Two reasons!

The first and most obvious is the compartmentalising of God. I believe in a limitless divine, and I mean that in every aspect. To accept any kind of certainty, any kind of accurate and definite definition of the divine is, you guessed it, immediately limiting the essential elements of that divine to that definition. It is immediately invalidated, for me anyway, and to accept such a certain definition would rob me of a notion which I will discuss shortly.

The second reason it would be spiritually deficient is the inherent notion of the limitless divine being transcendent; of humanity, mortality, time and space. This transcendence, vitally important to me, must surely be jettisoned if the certain make-up of God is understandable and containable within human cognisance. The very power of the limitless divine lies, at least in part, with the fact that we can NEVER have certainty as to its make-up. It is meant to be within us and our surroundings, and I believe it is, it is meant to be immanent, but also beyond. The awe and wonder that morphs an intellectual philosophy into an experiential faith exists exactly because we cannot define, or limit, or, let's face it, really ever 'know' God. We reach out with shaking or longing fingers, able to touch some, but never all of the limitless divine. The moment we reach out and know for certain we have grasped the 'all', is a moment beyond this lifetime. Oh and, of course, there is one other problem with certainty. In so many aspects of life, not just faith, it is the concept that one is right and thus the other wrong, that causes so much conflict. The notion that I have within my personal ambit the 'correct', the 'truth', embraced and guarded with paranoid righteousness is the cause of personal antagonism throughout the centuries. Why, on earth, would I want the limitless divine to be subject to and a part of such squalid human enmity!

Instead of certainty, we should strive to have a tryst with mystery. Accepting the notion we can never know for certain the limitless divine, though we experience the seismic aftershocks of our relationship with it, we acknowledge that nobody can claim 'right'. The limitless divine cannot be placed in a box, or a book for that matter, cannot be compartmentalised or squashed and twisted into mortal and human cognisance to satiate our arrogant desire to nail God down, no pun intended! The limitless divine pulses and spins in infinity with such glorious disparate and diverse reflections and interpretations of it because of a lack of certainty, not the other way around. It is the mystery of God which makes God! Yet we fight against it! Let us stop. Let us embrace the un-certainty. Let us move our feet on this earth in rhythmic joy that the divine is indeed limitless! Let us sing to the heavens that we do not have a God able to be shackled to the parameters of human cognisance, but willing to join us in song within our hearts and souls.

Let us actively engage in a tryst with mystery, and allow our faiths to soar beyond the certain.

Islam teaches us God is vast and one way we express this is reciting the '99 Names of Allah', Allah being the Arabic word for God. I remember how shocked I was when I first heard this; it was explained that an Arabic speaking Christian would refer to God as 'Allah'. I found this very confronting as I had been raised on the stereotypical mix of Islam vs the World, being indoctrinated with statements like 'Muslims pray to a different God'. So to find He was the same God I had been connected to my whole life and that the Lebanese Nun who had been my Grade 1 teacher would have called Him Allah was at first a little too much to handle. Merciful, Loving, Forgiving, were not words that I had associated with this Allah in my youth but unfolding before me in the pages of the Quran there He was: my God, my Strength, my Warmth, my Compassion and I Embraced Him with all my heart and soul.

But what do all these words really mean?

Allah knows me better than anyone; I can turn to him without fear of being judged. He is in the essence of my soul and in the wonder I feel when I look into my child's face. To me He is the beginning and the end – with all the love, tears, fear and laughter in between. He is an idea, a thought, a desire, an ambition, a dream and safe place to land. He is the reason I can cope in the shadows and my guiding light in the darkness, the brightness of the daylight, the dampness of the rainforest and the scorching heat of the Australian sun, but most of all He is my compass, for without him I would lose my way. As a child feels safe with the boundaries its parents give it, so too do I. Instead of an 'out of control' view of the world where we seem to be hurtling along from birth to death, a belief in a higher power gives me a sense of order and meaning. Not one of the controller or magician pulling our strings but a hand to guide and sustain me through my journey.

'I would lose my way' – is that really so or just a dramatic statement because I am caught up in the moment? Are those who do not believe lost? No. We are all called in different ways and each one has their own journey, their path, I have chosen mine and God does not teach me to judge others for their choice, but respect and learn.

"O mankind! We created you from a single (pair) of a male and a female, and made you into nations and tribes, that ye may know each other (not that ye may despise (each other)." Quran 49:13

This verse sums it all up for me. I believe God is the one who challenges me every day to be my best self, to live my best life and when inevitably at times I fail miserably teaches me not to be too hard on myself for He if he can forgive me then who am I not to forgive myself?

Sikhs believe in worshipping One God (*Puja Akal Ki*) who lives everywhere and in the hearts of all.

The Sikh religion is strictly monotheistic, believing in one supreme God, free of gender, absolute, all pervading, eternal Creator. This universal God of love is obtained through grace, sought by service to mankind. These were the first teachings of Guru Nanak, the founder of the faith. The Sikh faith views life as a unique opportunity to discover and develop the divinity in each of us.

Sikhs believe different religions are different paths to realize God. Sikhi asserts the individual's right to commune directly with God regardless of status, caste or religion. Sikhs believe in one universal God. This is the core teaching of the Sikh Holy Scripture, Sri Guru Granth Sahib, the eternal Guru of the Sikhs. Compiled by the Gurus during their lifetime, it is co-authored by persons of many faiths. A Sikh respects and accepts all other world religions and protects and allows the free-practice of the customs and rituals of other religions.

The twelve words at the beginning of the Guru Granth Sahib are the most widely known by Sikhs. With the brevity of a text message, they sum up Guru Nanak's essential teaching. The opening affirmation '*ik oangkar*' means 'There is one god', 'one reality'.

From the rest of this introduction to the Guru Granth Sahib, a monotheistic view of God emerges. The emphasis is on 'one'. In the original, *Ek* (one) is written not as a word but as a numeral, so emphasizing the singularity, uniqueness, and indivisibility of *Oangkar*. Similarly, *Oangkar* is represented as an alphabetic character, one nasalized vowel that encapsulates the universe's vibration in a single resonant syllable.

The remaining ten words mean truth by name, the creator, without fear, without hate, timeless in form, beyond birth, self existent, discovered by the grace of the Guru.

Mool mantar is the name of these twelve words. A *mantar* (mantra) is an empowering formula for repetition; *mool* means a root. The whole of the Guru's teaching (and of Sikh spirituality) grows from and draws sustenance from this statement. Guru Nanak's longer compositions develop upon this theme, and provide the basis of Sikh theology.

Truth is supreme and with this God is equated. The lines of the Japji Sahib which immediately follow the *mool mantar* emphasize this:

Truth in the beginning
Truth when time began
Truth even now and for always

At the same time, God is the creator actively participating in the world. God does not, however, intervene in the world's affairs by means of incarnation. Ram, Mohan (a way of addressing Krishna), and Hari (the title 'Lord' often given by Hindus to Rama and Krishna) recur in the hymns of Guru Nanak as ways of referring to the divine. So too do the Hindu names Shiv (Shiva), Braham (Brahma), and Paramatma (supreme soul), together with words from Islam for God – Allah, Rabb, Khuda, and Sahib.

God, the ultimate reality, is *sargun* (possessing all attributes), as well as being *nirgun* (beyond all attributes). The divine is invisible (*alakh*) and formless (*nirankar*). God is also *niranjan* (literally, 'unsmudged with eyeliner'), that is, unentangled in illusion (*maya*).

Following immediately after the m*ool mantar*, Guru Nanak's Japji celebrates cosmic order and divine will, a concept he called *hukam*. It is through the divine will that everything exists, and to *hukam* everyone should submit.

The *hukam* of creation reveals God, and so too does *shabad*, the word, in the sense of divine revelation, and *naam*, the name. *Naam* is central to Guru Nanak's teaching, as it means not only the word or utterance through which truth is revealed, but is itself the compression or encapsulation of divine reality. *Naam* is for Guru Nanak the total divine self-expression, rather than merely God's title, and on its power human life depends.

Guru Nanak communicates the immediacy of God through images, for example:

> You are the ocean, all-knowing, all-seeing.
> How can I, a fish, perceive your limits?
> Wherever I look, there you are.
> If I leave you I burst and die.
> (GGS:25)

Guru Nanak emphasized the oneness of God, the supreme creator, a God of love. Men and women, he said, should not fear God's anger but be afraid of not receiving all the benefits of his love.

The approach to God within the Theravada Buddhist tradition is subtle and complex. By the term 'God', I understand the concept of an all-knowing, all-powerful creator deity. In this way, this question is perhaps more suited to monotheistic religious traditions in which a single God is pivotal to notions of salvation and liberation. In Theravada Buddhism, however, the idea of 'God' is largely irrelevant.

Within the Theravada tradition, the ultimate reality is an impersonal state known as *nirvana*, an unchanging, blissful object of liberation. Its attainment is characterised by the complete end of all suffering, the goal of the Theravada Buddhist tradition. In attaining *nirvana* it is not necessary to rely on the existence of a God since liberation is the fruit of an individual's actions. *Nirvana* is not a state that can be granted by another being but is a state that is attained only when someone extinguishes once and for all the fires of greed, hatred and delusion. According to the tradition, these three fires perpetuate our suffering and separate us from liberation. It is only when we realise this existence, supported by greed, hatred and delusion, causes us to suffer, is impermanent and has no independent nature that we reject its supports and turn towards enlightenment.

This turn towards enlightenment, the path to end all suffering, is known as the eight-fold path and comprises of 1) Right View, 2) Right Intention, 3) Right Speech, 4) Right Action, 5) Right Livelihood, 6) Right Effort, 7) Right Mindfulness and 8) Right Concentration. This path can be divided into three sections, with numbers 1 and 2 representing the development of wisdom, 3, 4 and 5 representing the development of ethical conduct, and 6, 7 and 8 representing mental development or meditation. Therefore, the path to liberation is a balance of wisdom, morality and meditation. All three are interdependent and enlightenment cannot exist without all being present.

The realisation of ultimate reality, the end of suffering, in Theravada Buddhism does not necessitate the existence of an all-knowing, all-powerful creator deity as our own actions define our future existence. There is no personal judgement by another being and grace is not necessary for liberation. This is not to say that in Theravada Buddhist cultures there is not a belief in a variety of beings and levels of reality. There are many heavens filled with powerful deities. However, these deities are not creators of existence and are not all-knowing and all-powerful. They are subject to the same suffering and impermanence as we are and they too will die and be reborn. In Theravada Buddhism there is no divine being that can grant liberation. In this way, the attainment of *nirvana* does not require a God. Therefore, Theravada Buddhism is perhaps unique in that it is not theistic, atheistic or agnostic. It is simply not necessary to have a position at all!

What can one learn about God? And how can such knowledge be gained? These are among the most important questions on the path of spiritual search.

Bahá'ís believe that God is eternal, omniscient, and conscious of His[3] creation. God's signs and attributes are reflected in creation, but the essence of God is unseen, inaccessible, and unknowable to human beings. Because God is unlimited and infinite, but the human mind is limited and finite, human beings cannot *"comprehend the eternal, unmanifest Creator"*[4]. Just as a painting lacks the capacity to understand the artist who painted it, so it is not possible for humanity to understand the essence of God, the Creator of all.

The Bahá'í scriptures explain that because we as human beings cannot directly access and know God, He has in each age sent a pure and stainless soul who has acted as an intermediary between God and humanity. God has provided this connection to Himself because of His love for humanity. These intermediaries (or "Manifestations of God") have included such historical figures as Krishna, Buddha, Zoroaster, Abraham, Moses, Christ,

Muhammad, the Báb and Bahá'u'lláh. They have been the founders of the world's great religions. The Manifestations are God's representatives – "mirrors that truly and faithfully reflect the light of God"[5]. Although God's essence will forever remain unknowable to the human mind, God's qualities – such as love, mercy, knowledge and power – may be known through the Manifestations who perfectly reflect these divine attributes: "In the Manifestation of God, the perfectly polished mirror, appear the qualities of the Divine in a form that man is capable of comprehending"[6].

The analogy of the sun shining in a mirror helps to explain the relationship of God, the Manifestation, and humanity. God is like the sun, which is the source of life but which can never be closely approached or fully understood by any human being. The Manifestation of God is like a perfectly polished mirror that reflects the sun's light. Just as by turning towards the mirror, one is able to see the image of the sun, by turning toward the mirror of the Manifestation, one is able to see the spiritual image of God.

Bahá'u'lláh wrote that everything in creation is God's handiwork and therefore reflects something of His attributes. For example, even in the intimate structure of a rock or a crystal can be seen the order of God's creation. However, the more refined the object, the more completely is it capable of reflecting God's attributes. Since the Manifestation of God is the highest form of creation known to us, it is in the lives of the Manifestations that the deeper meaning of God's attributes can be most perfectly understood. God is not limited by a physical body, and so we cannot see Him directly or observe His personality. Hence our knowledge of the Manifestation is, in fact, the closest we can come to the knowledge of God.

"The door of the knowledge of the Ancient Being [God] hath ever been, and will continue to be, closed in the face of men. No man's understanding shall ever gain access unto His holy court. As a token of His mercy, however, and as a proof of His loving-kindness, He hath manifested unto men the Day Stars of His divine guidance, the Symbols of His divine unity, and hath ordained the knowledge of these sanctified Beings to be identical with the knowledge of His own Self."[7]

Of course, only those who live during the time of a Manifestation have the opportunity of observing Him directly. It is for this reason, Bahá'u'lláh explained, that the essential connection between the individual and God is maintained through the writings and words of each Manifestation. For Bahá'ís, the word of the Manifestation is the Word of God, and it is to this Word that the individual can turn in his or her daily life in order to grow closer to God and to acquire a deeper knowledge of Him. The written Word of God is the instrument that creates a consciousness of God's presence in one's daily life:

"Say: The first and foremost testimony establishing His truth is His own Self. Next to this testimony is His Revelation. For whoso faileth to recognize either the one or the other He hath established the words He hath revealed as proof of His reality and truth.... He hath endowed every soul with the capacity to recognize the signs of God."[8]

It is for this reason that the discipline of daily prayer, meditation, and study of the holy writings constitutes an important part of the individual spiritual practice of Bahá'ís. They feel that this discipline is one of the most important ways of growing closer to their Creator.

To summarize: the Bahá'í view of God is that His essence is eternally transcendent, but that His attributes and qualities are completely immanent in the Manifestations. Since our knowledge of anything is limited to our knowledge of the perceptible attributes of that thing, knowledge of the

Manifestations is (for ordinary humans) equivalent to knowledge of God.[9] In practical terms, this knowledge is gained through study, prayer, meditation and practical application based on the revealed Word of God (i.e., the sacred scriptures of the Manifestations).[10]

God for me is a moving target. Although I am theoretically a fan of systematic theologies, I will openly confess that there is nothing systematic about my personal theology at all. Quite simply, I need to believe that God is present in my life—that God is sustaining and guiding me, particularly at the most trying moments. At the same time, I refuse to hold God responsible for misfortune and tragedy. My God must always be good, even when that is inconsistent with my desperate hope that God has the power to look after those I love most dearly.

The ancient rabbis told a powerful myth: when the Romans destroyed the Holy Temple in the year 70 C.E. (Common Era), the Jews were sent into a sad and bitter exile. They had been cut off from all that was important to them—their central place of worship, and their holy land. According to the rabbis, when the Jews went into exile, an aspect of God went into exile along with them. This part of God was not the mighty creator and destroyer responsible for all the miracles in the Bible. Instead, this was the aspect of God which dwelled most closely to human beings. In Hebrew this aspect is known as *Shekhinah*, meaning 'one who dwells within or close by'. I should emphasise that this term was later reworked by the medieval kabbalists to mean something quite different. The meaning that I am focusing on is that of the rabbis of 2000 years ago, who took comfort in the idea that, at the time of their greatest tragedy, the Jews were accompanied and held by God.

These same rabbis portrayed God as having multiple personalities: kind, judgmental, loving and vindictive. As I've said, I am very selective in how I portray God. God is all love, all kindness, all care. The universe can be a frightening and unpredictable place, but God for me is an ongoing source of comfort and reassurance.

The traditional Mahāyāna answer, like that of modern process theologians, is that there is no God in the classical theistic sense (omnipotent, omniscient, omnibenevolent). However, the Mahāyāna tradition teaches of a transcendent and compassionate Presence that invites all beings to be saved. Mahāyāna envisages this as the Buddha in his three bodies (trikāya).[11] The first body is his Body of Truth (dharmakāya), which embodies the causal and moral order of reality as well as the principle of Dharma and enlightenment. The second is the Body of Bliss (sambhogakāya), which manifests Buddhas and bodhisattvas controlling universes called Pure Lands or Buddha-fields (buddhakAektra).[12] The third is the Manifestation Body (nirmanakāya), of whom the most important was our world-system's Śākyamuni, the historical sage who lived 2500 years ago in ancient India. All Buddhas and bodhisattvas share the Body of Truth, although their outward manifestations in the sambhogakāya and nirmanakāya may be different. Their multiplicity is their strength, or so the Mahāyāna teaches. Buddhas and bodhisattvas employ countless skilful means (*upāya*) to guide beings to the teachings of wisdom and compassion. Through infinitely diverse forms and methods they act in tandem to save the worlds' creatures.

In the *Flower Ornament Scripture* (*AvataAsaka sūtra*), the Buddha[13] is seen to be present throughout the universe in the same way the universe is present in a single atom. The light of all Buddhas is commonly described as being infinite, illuminating the worlds of the "ten directions." The *Flower Ornament Scripture* posits the cosmos itself as the Pure Land of the Buddha. While I hesitate to ascribe the usual descriptive categories in philosophy of religion to these beliefs (such as pantheism, monism, etc.), I do think they share a degree of common ground with the theistic idea of immanence (as noted, *saAsāra* is no different to *NirvāAa*), while at the same time maintaining their transcendent distinction (as a normal being, I'm dreadfully far from being enlightened!).

To be clear, almost all Buddhist schools have a concept of the Buddha's transcendent nature, which is beyond words, doctrinal formulations and conceptual thinking. However, it is the Mahāyāna that posits a "womb" of Buddhahood, or Buddha-matrix, that is inherent in every being (this is known as *tathāgata-garbha* tradition). This is an affirming vision, one that insists on the potential goodness and potential that is too often obscured by mental defilements and impurities. In the final Mahāyāna analysis, all beings are Buddhas and must therefore be respected and treated as such.

God is a phrase used to describe the indescribable, ineffable, omnipotent, omniscient force that permeates all life on earth.

God is the connective energy that holds all pieces of the Universe together. God resides inside each person and throughout every creature and all forms of matter. That which is God is connected to thought, emotion, desire and ego, and to the highest levels of consciousness of all beings. God inhabits many forms and all God forms that have been imagined are varying ideas on the same principle or life-force. The idea of God is so vast and our understanding of the concept is so difficult that we imagine and create smaller Gods that resonate within our lives and the lessons important to each individual's development. God leads us to ourselves, to each other, and the connection with all life.

God in the broadest Pagan lens is seen as the Divinity immanent within the creation; or rather there is a direct and immediate continuum between Creator and Creation rendering the distinction moot. All things are Divine; all things are part and parcel of God; and God is within all things. Pagan theology (or even theology[14]) is as varied as the diversity inherent in our communities. We are animists, pantheists, polytheists, archetypists (i.e. Jungian psychology), monists, henotheistic monotheists and ditheists, and often all of the above simultaneously. We regard each theological lens as a map, which we attempt to never confuse with the territory. Our traditions encourage us as Pagans to perceive/experience first and believe later. In fact, to describe any strain of Paganism as an orthodoxy (uniformity of doctrine or belief) would be a difficult feat. It is much easier to identify orthopraxy (uniformity of practice) within our traditions.

Personally I draw a distinction between that which many

religious and faith traditions call 'God' and what Pagans name 'deities'. I feel that all is woven into the fabric of God Herself (the Weaver or the Star Goddess) and that within Her Body and Being is an endless multiplicity of spirits. Some of these spirits or embodied forces (like 'fire' or 'river') are so vital and powerful that they become deep and necessary potencies that act as agencies or catalysts within the continuum of creativity. These 'hidden' potencies are the deities we Pagans often call Gods and Goddesses and they are as real as you or me; in fact each of us has the potential to become a deity – a living God or Goddess. Many of the ancient Pagan cultures (e.g. the Celtic) viewed their deities as their glorious ancestors. The Yoruban cultures of West Africa also point to the origin of their Orisha within the ancestral legacy.

To say that Pagans believe in or worship One Supreme Power would be incorrect (although some would); however to say that Pagans believe in, revere and work with an Intelligence, a Presence and a Being with which we are identified, is testament to our deep philosophies. The Principle of Sacred Equality – that all share in equal worth and in the same authority – gives justice to the Zero (the Centre and the Circumference) who/which nurtures and dissolves all things.

It should be mentioned that it is the inclination of many Pagans to refer to the Divine as feminine (not necessarily as gendered 'female'), but rarely to the exclusion of the masculine. This is partly because we live in an overwhelmingly patriarchal society that suppresses and denigrates the feminine and has done so for the past 3000 years. By referring to the 'Goddess' or the 'Mother', we are recreating a balance and addressing a deep wound within our collective cultural psyche. Another reason for referring to the Divine as feminine is because psychologically and emotionally our first human experience is connected to our birth from our mothers. This is an experience we all have in common. However, Paganism embraces both masculine and feminine images of divinity, as well as those which are androgynous or non-gendered.

"Holy Mother, in you we live, move and have our being. From you all things emerge, and unto you all things return." (An Anderson Feri Prayer to the Star Goddess)

God is an impossible term to define. Where does one begin? I suppose the very first thing to say is that God is a metaphor and all God-language is metaphorical. Think of some of the terms we (people of faith) use in reference to 'God' – Father, Mother, Child, Gate, Doorway, Lion, Lamb, Son of God, Divine Artist, Vine, Life etc. These are all metaphors and many of them are *anthropomorphic* metaphors. We use them because all we have to interpret and make sense of the Divine are our own human experiences. We use terms like Mother and Father because, as children, our own parents were god-like figures to us. They were the ones who cared for us, fed us, clothed us, held us when we were hurt and punished us when we were naughty. They seemed all powerful. They knew what to do.

I say this at the start because I truly believe that if we really understood how all God language is metaphorical there would be far less religious falling out and fighting. In fact it would end religious warfare. If we knew that our God-language was simply a metaphor for an experience, we would not say things like, 'My God is the only true God.' We would know that everyone's picture of God is culturally defined and is moulded by experience.

So for me the more important question is not 'What is God?' but 'What is *not* God.'

As a panentheist I would say that pretty much everything is part of 'God.' One of my great heroes of the faith is Matthew Fox who often now refers to god as 'Life' for it's a whole lot harder to project on life. The problem with the metaphors we have traditionally used – like Father, King, Almighty etc. – is that they are so easily projected upon and the God we believe in becomes just a mirror of ourselves. Not only that it often becomes a mirror and a projection of our shadow side, so 'God' becomes a great judge in the sky because we are judgemental and so on.

I can see already that I'm not really answering the question but this is where I currently am in my thinking. However I suppose I ought to try and answer the actual question which, I guess, is far more to do with whether I actually believe there to be a reality behind all that myth and metaphor and, if so, what do I understand it to be like.

Well first off – I'm not a non-realist. I respect non-realism and am challenged by it but, for me, when I say that all God language is metaphorical that does not necessarily mean that I see 'God' is an abstract concept and not an actual reality.

The myriad of god images (be they the monotheist Yahweh or the polytheistic Persephone or Pan) are metaphors for *actual* experiences of *actual* realities. I cannot see it any other way. God – the Great All – is a real presence in and through and beyond all things. That's how I've always understood it and I can't really see that changing. I once wrote about the Great Mosaic (another metaphor) which is the great picture we humans have made by coming up with our own images and interpretation of the divine. Each of our pictures is like a small coloured stone within the great mosaic of the Divine ALL.

God is a fairly uninvolved concept. God as a creator is accepted in Vodou, but God as an accessible being is not. The Vodou idea of God is based on the African model. In many African religions, particularly those from the Ivory Coast and the Bight of Benin, from which areas Vodou stems, there is a belief that God or a God-like figure created the world and then, usually in conjunction with others (either His children or fellow Gods), he created animals, people, and things. Following this great act of Creation, he withdrew from the affairs of the world to exist in a state of rest and contemplation for the rest of eternity.

The overriding idea is that the concept of God is vast—too huge to be concerned with the problems of the beings he created. He did not create the world so that he could care for it; he created the world so that it could exist. For this reason, God is viewed in the Vodou religion as a creator being, not a loving God.

While God is remote and largely irrelevant to the daily lives of humankind, the *lwa*, or spirits, are actively engaged. They exist in a plane between humans and God, and have access to knowledge and power that can help or guide their human communities. They were once humans, ancestors of Vodounists today, though they have become much more than that. The *lwa* are often compared to Catholic saints, however this is a super-ficial and problematic comparison. The *lwa* do not hold any direct connection to God, although it is understood that they may have access to all spiritual realms, including the one in which God exists.

As the *lwa* were once human, they retain many of their human characteristics. This means that they are not like 'heavenly beings' with only pure intentions. They are very human in many ways, and are prone to impatience, mischief or even disinterest, though they are susceptible to flattery and willingly accept gifts or sacrifice in exchange for ongoing guidance. Their humanity also creates a stronger connection between them and a particular community, and also to individuals. It is common for Vodounists to have one or two *maît-tête*, or those who live 'in their head'. It is to these *lwa* that most Vodounists will turn, rather than God, when they need guidance.

Firstly, in the Celtic Pagan traditions "God" is not singular and is experienced as both female and male.

Goddesses and Gods manifest in a myriad of shape-changing forms. Therefore the pantheon of Celtic Gods is not static but forms an ever-changing, fluid and polytheistic cosmology. This shape-changing ability extends to the poets and heroes of Celtic mythological history (or as some prefer, historical mythology) as well as to their Divine beings. As such it is one of the fundamentals necessary to understanding the Celtic world view.

This transformational ability comes in three forms (three being a sacred number in Celtic numerology). Metamorphosis occurs when a being changes form – from human, to animal, to fish, to vegetation, to elements and back again. Metempsychosis occurs when a being passes from one body to another after death. Reincarnation occurs when a being is reborn. These transformational abilities are common elements in the mythologies of Ireland, Britain, Wales and Scotland.

This form of aspectual deity is very different from the classical representations of Gods and Goddesses in Egypt, Greece and Rome. In pre-Roman Britain, Celtic deities were represented symbolically. It is only after the Roman conquest and the rise of Romano-Celtic society that representational images are found. In Ireland, where there was no conquest, the sacred places are marked by symbols – the triple spiral of Newgrange is one of the oldest and most beautiful representations of the Triple Goddess. The understanding of this type of God has all but been forgotten in Western civilization, though it is found in the Gods and Goddesses of India – both in pre-Vedic and Vedic antiquity and in modern Hinduism. The closest parallel in today's Western civilization is the understanding of the three-in-one Christian Trinity.

The Divine in Celtic Paganism is both immanent and transcendent. Simply, this means that it is found within all elements of the natural world (immanent) while at the same time all elements of the natural world are part of a Divinity that transcends and is greater than the sum of its parts. 'God' is found within every living creature and also in the very elements of the landscape itself. The *dindsenchas* of Ireland are the place-naming stories which connect the Gods to the land and its formations – especially rivers, springs, wells, mountains and caves.

The Celtic Pagan Goddess is not understood as the Creator of the cosmos but as the soul or spirit which gives life to the physical elements of the natural world – earth, air, fire and water – that are the chemical building blocks of life. Rather than being seen as a potter who has made a beautiful pot, or a watchmaker who has manufactured a magnificent time-piece (creator and created who are distinct and separate from each other), She is seen as the Great Mother of the world. That world is both a separate entity from Her but at the same time is part of Her and composed of the same elements and with the same life force that flows through Her. She is not 'out there' looking down on us; she is within each and every one of us, and every one of us is part of

Her. It is through this belief that Celtic Pagans embrace Panentheism. We do not worship rocks and trees as 'Gods', but we do recognise and honour the divine elements that are embodied in and are visible in the earth and all of its creatures. This Panentheistic world view continued into Celtic Christianity as well.

This embracing of Panentheism enables us to experience true awe and wonder when we are faced with the magnificence of the natural world and its breath-taking phenomena. From majestic mountains to the scales on the wing of a butterfly; from the unimaginable creatures of the deepest oceans to the soaring beauty of the greatest eagles; from the incredible delicacy and intricacy of microscopic life to the truly inspiring light and magic of a spiral nebula – our 'God' is manifest. This awe and wonder, in turn, enables us to truly appreciate the complex interconnected web of life that is apparent in the totality of every single thing that is part of this world and is the basis of the relationship that each individual has to every other being – animal, vegetable and mineral – on this planet, and by extension to the very limits of the cosmos. Truly, for a Celtic Pagan 'God' is everywhere.

The Celtic pantheon is one way of explaining and under-standing this kind of Divinity. The first among the Celtic Pagan Goddesses is the Great Mother. Historically, Her roots go back many thousands of years – some believe as far back as 10,000 years before the Common Era. Initially She was the head of her tribe and leader of Her people. The Great Mother is a triple Goddess (again the sacred number three), as are many Celtic Goddesses, Her three aspects being life, fertility and death. She is also known as the Goddess of Sovereignty or the Goddess of the Land, personifying the land itself, its fertility and the prosperity of the tribe. In this aspect She is of prime importance to Celtic Kingship as a would-be King must be married to the Land he seeks to rule. She also represents the three ages of women – maidenhood, motherhood and old age – the times of youthful strength, nurturing and caring, and the revered wisdom of those who were fortunate enough to reach old age and pass on the knowledge of the ancestors as well as of their own life experiences. She is known by many names in different places, each tribe having their own name for Her. Many of these names have been lost as the Celtic tradition was an oral tradition and because tribal members were protective of their Goddesses and Gods and would 'Swear by the Gods my people swear by' rather than name their deities to those outside their clan. As with many of the oldest deities, She is known more usually by Her title, though the name Danu has been used in Ireland and Don in Britain.

The first among the Celtic Gods is the Great Father, the Father of All or the Good God. He has a great knowledge of all things, oversees the weather elements and the harvest, and can perform great feats of strength and endurance. The name the Dagda has come down through history for Him, and He is consort to the Great Mother. Other archetypal Gods and Goddesses (and there are hundreds of them) include the Youthful God (Oengus, Mabon), the Old Veiled One (Cailleach, the Morrighan), and the Bright One (Lugh, Llew), but it must be remembered that these are all aspects and manifestations of the divinity which is the world in which we dwell and with which we are interconnected.

CHAPTER TWO

What is Faith?

Faith is a word I rarely use to describe my spirituality. However within the broader context of interfaith or interreligious dialogue I can see the meaning of the word as implicit, rather than as overt.

A faith tradition is akin to a religious or spiritual tradition. Due to my love of etymology, the study of the origins and development of words, I understand concepts via their evolution. To have faith is to have hope, or trust in something beyond or something immanent (the eternal Divine paradox). To be religious is to desire to re-link (with [the] God/s), make sacred (sacrifice) or to adhere. Spirituality is a broad term which tends to be the most effective in communicating the ideals of those who would use the word – to honour the Spirit.

When it comes to Paganism and our varied traditions and groupings, the words religion and spirituality are generally favoured over 'faith'. There seems to be a knee-jerk reaction against the word because it may imply 'blind faith' which is an unspoken tenet of the dogmatic fundamentalist interpretations of major religions. Paganism does not encourage blind faith in anything; we are much more comfortable with the concept of trust and autonomous authority. We place faith in the Divinity of All Things and in our own personal sacred natures and thus we are opened to the idea that all the wisdom of the cosmos lies also within each of us. Thus to have faith is to make use of not only the intuitive faculties, but also the intellect, and to fuse these together to pursue that which is beheld by neither, but the reason for both.

In a Pagan sense, to have faith is to actively engage with the principles of 'perfect love and perfect trust' which are the passwords of initiation in many Wiccan and Witchcraft groups. The ideals of perfect love and perfect trust are not absolutes; we do not pretend to perfection, we aspire towards the wholeness of it, and we understand that this must always be worked toward as there is no end to their expression and depth. I articulate spiritual engagement as deepening thresholds which I call Self, Community and Cosmos. First and foremost we must cultivate faith in Self, then only can we extend the works of Faith to our human and non-human communities (the latter component is just as essential, as we are nothing without the non-human). To build active faith in our community ('shared unity') we then reach the 'level' of Cosmos and universal aspects begin to emerge. The Holy Mystery in Cosmos is that when we can truly see 'Self' reflected in 'Cosmos' and 'Cosmos' embodied within 'Self' we have attained to Gnosis of Personal Godhood – we have actualised our Divinity. We have come to Own Holy Self and when this is activated or acted from we cultivate Sovereignty of Self, which is also known as Self-Possession. In doing this we are no longer in the realms of faith; we have become authentic; and yet faith in Self has opened this most important door for us.

For the Buddhist, faith has two characteristics. It causes the mind to become composed and settled, and it inspires it with the confidence to embark and continue on the spiritual journey. It serves a crucial function by arousing the individual to not just theorize and debate about, but study, apply and practice the Buddha's teachings. It empowers and motivates, and is a self-renewing wellspring of healing and encouragement. While the Buddha may have denied that faith and rituals alone can bring about the cessation of suffering, all traditions no doubt teach that faith is a preliminary virtue that is essential throughout the Buddhist way of life. Theravāda Buddhism is commonly perceived as the most "rational" or "secular" of all the traditions, whilst both Buddhologists and popular writers have sometimes seen Mahāyāna as the more devotional strain. From the beginning, however, both Theravāda *and* Mahāyāna have insisted on the need for faith as well as intellectual engagement.

At its most basic, faith is a trustful confidence (*śraddhā*) in the truth and veracity of the Dharma, the cosmic and uncreated law that accounts for causality, moral accountability and spiritual progress. This faith is established by encountering a Buddha (which is seen as a very rare opportunity) who has discovered this Dharma and revealed it to humanity. In the Mahāyāna, this faith expands to encompass faith in the pantheon of Buddhas and bodhisattvas that populate the Buddhist multiverse. As the focus of devotion and worship, these divine beings in manifold world-systems can be prayed and confessed to, revered and adulated. They do not demand obedience, although it is obviously spiritually prudent to follow their teachings and allow oneself to be guided by their wisdom. As the needs of each sentient being will be unique, faith must be accommodated and cultivated in a multiplicity of different ways.

Faith is not, as it is often construed, merely a comfort blanket for poor deluded religious people. Indeed, faith in Mahāyāna Buddhism challenges us to *dare* to believe that no matter how cruel, evil, or vain humanity seems, we are actually all latent Buddhas.[15] Perhaps most strikingly, this also means that even the blackest of personalities can be redeemed: if not in this life, then in many, many future lives to come. Due to philosophical divergences, other religions don't allow the possibility of endless chances, but Mahāyāna remains an advocate of this doctrinal position. The bodhisattva never turns his back or gives up even though the sins of beings (and beings themselves) are innumerable. This lofty faith is encapsulated in the Bodhisattva Vow, which can be taken by both laypeople and the monastic community. For me, it is the quintessential inspiration of the Mahāyāna Buddhist's faith in herself and others:

"From now onwards, I will practice generosity, however small, protect morality, show forbearance, act with vigour, practice meditation, and adhere to wisdom. I will train in all the roots of merit, and I will apply them all for the sake, benefit and happiness of all living beings, and for gaining the highest and perfect enlightenment."

Bodhibhadra, *BodhisattvasaAvaravidhi*[16]

Faith is a strong belief in God and in the doctrines of a religion, based on spiritual apprehension rather than scientific proof. It is an inner perception of the soul which goes beyond purely rational external arguments. It is an inner certitude that, despite our inability to fully understand the manifold aspects of reality, there is a loving Creator and a divine plan for creation. We may sense it most fully in times of contemplation and prayer:

"…if the inner perception be open, a hundred thousand clear proofs become visible … when man feels the indwelling spirit, he is in no need of arguments for its existence…"[17]

Faith is unique to each individual and is tied to one's personal insights, efforts and experiences. Faith is born when the heart recognises the love of God. As one walks in the path of Faith, through tests and confirmations, one's love for God grows.

> "The emancipated soul sees with the eyes of perfect faith because it knows that vast provisions are made to enable it to gain the victory over every difficulty and trial. Yet man must ever remember, the earth plane is a workshop and not an art gallery for the exhibition of powers. This is not the plane of perfection, but earth is the crucible for refining and moulding character."[18]

Bahá'u'lláh teaches that true Faith is expressed through action:

> "…the essence of faith is fewness of words and abundance of deeds…"[19]

But how should these deeds be guided? Bahá'ís believe that we learn of God's will through the teachings of the Manifestations of God. Hence each Bahá'í strives to study and meditate on those teachings and how they relate to the events in our lives. Bahá'u'lláh tells us that we are to consult with trusted friends about our understanding of these teachings and their application to various situations that arise. At a community level, consultation at Bahá'í gatherings is used to determine plans of action which are then carried out in a spirit of unity with the goal of carrying forward an ever-advancing civilisation. Whether in terms of spiritual practice, moral behaviour, social activism or community participation, Bahá'ís seek to continually improve themselves and the world around them.

> "It is incumbent upon every man of insight to strive to

translate that which hath been written into reality and action...."[20]

Striving to put the teachings of the Manifestations into practice in our lives can be challenging, as there are many demands and pressures which can lead us away from the right path. It is easy to get distracted by *the hosts of idle fancies and vain imaginations*[21] The practices of prayer, meditation and consultation can help to keep us on the right track.

A good description of how, at the individual level, we can put faith into action to overcome problems is described in the following passage:

"Use these five steps if we have a problem of any kind for which we desire a solution, or wish help.

Pray and meditate about it. Use the prayers of the Manifestations, as they have the greatest power. Learn to remain in the silence of contemplation for a few moments. During this deepest communion take the next step.

Arrive at a decision and hold to this. This decision is usually born in a flash at the close or during the contemplation. It may seem almost impossible of accomplishment, but if it seems to be an answer to prayer or a way of solving the problem, then immediately take the next step.

Have determination to carry the decision through. Many fail here. The decision, budding into determination, is blighted and instead becomes a wish or a vague longing. When determination is born, immediately take the next step.

Have faith and confidence, that the Power of the Holy Spirit will flow through you, the right way will appear, the door will open, the right message, the right principle or the right book will be given to you. Have confidence, and the right thing will come to meet your need. Then as you rise from prayer take immediately the fifth step.

Act as though it had all been answered. Then act with tireless, ceaseless energy. And, as you act, you yourself will become a magnet which will attract more power to your being, until you become an unobstructed channel for the Divine Power to flow through you".[22]

Faith is trusting that even though you as an individual are unable to see all of the ramifications of your actions, if you strive to live according to the teachings of the Manifestations your efforts will ultimately be blessed and bear fruit.

"Rely upon God. Trust in Him. Praise Him. Call Him continually to mind. He verily turneth trouble into ease and sorrow into solace, and toil into utter peace. He verily hath dominion over all things."[23]

"And now I give you a commandment which shall be as a covenant between you and Me – that ye have faith; that your faith be steadfast as a rock that no storms can move, that nothing can disturb, and that it endure through all things even to the end... As ye have faith, so shall your powers and blessings be. This is the balance this is the balance – this is the balance."[24]

For me, 'faith' is my absolute belief that the Divine is within each and every being on this planet as well as embodying and encompassing the Earth itself (and by extension the entire cosmos). I believe in the Earth and its place in the solar system (the third rock from the Sun); the solar system's place in the Milky Way; and our galaxy's place in the universe. I believe in the 23 degree tilt of the Earth's axis that gives us the Wheel of the Year and the seasons by which we measure their progressive cycle of life, death and rebirth.

I believe in the Celtic Pagan cycle of festivals and rituals that celebrate the Wheel of the Year. Like the Celtic day, which begins at sunset, the Celtic year begins as the Wheel turns towards winter; for the Celts understood that light comes from the darkness, and that new life quickens from the bare and barren earth of winter. They understood that the only constant is change and that the seed of its opposite is found within everything. The Wheel follows this cycle:

Samhain is the time when we honour our ancestors and give thanks for the knowledge they have passed down to us so we can prepare for the winter to come and plan for the future seasons.

This is followed by Yule, the Winter solstice, the longest night after which the Sun grows ever stronger with the promise of life to come. The Sun is also the Son of the Goddess in Celtic myth and His rebirth at the very depth of winter gave hope to the ancient people who depended on the crucial growing warmth for survival.

Imbolc, meaning 'in the belly', is when the land is prepared for new crops so that the belly of the Earth can bring forth new life. It is the time of lambing and the first early green shoots as the plants dormant during the winter cold are reborn.

Then comes the Spring equinox, Ostara, where day and night are balanced, seeds are sown and the fertile Earth celebrated. The growing strength of the Sun and the longer days bring increased energy for the work ahead.

Next comes the fire festival of Beltaine which celebrates the flourishing of nature – plants, animals and humans feel the growing energy and life force of the land. This is the time when thoughts and actions turn to joyous love and the fulfilment of the passion for life.

The Summer solstice, Litha, the time of light and the longest day celebrates the power of the Sun; it is a haven between the toil of planting and the toil of harvesting – a time of games and feasting and thanksgiving. It is also a turning point in the year, as from now light begins to ebb as the darkness grows. We are reminded that nothing is certain but change, which is the basis of life's cycles.

Lughnasagh is the festival of the first harvest, the first fruits of high summer that will provide for the coming seasons. We give thanks for the bountiful harvest as we realise that the days are growing shorter and that winter will soon return and we must make ready for the dark times to come.

Finally there is Mabon, the Autumnal equinox, the time of the second harvest that must be preserved for winter; a time when day and night are again in balance but this time it is the darkness that is increasing and we draw to the end of our year – to start all over again.

I believe that we are all linked together through the interconnected web of life. We do not live in isolation and this means that every action we take has a consequence, every cause has an effect, and more importantly it means that we must take responsibility for our actions and be accountable for the outcomes of those actions. The Celtic Pagan world-view understands and experiences nature as a whole. We live in a world where consciousness is inherent within the very fibres of existence and our actions cause ripples through that consciousness.

I believe that all life – human and non-human animals, and the elements that make up all the diverse environments that exist in this world – is sacred and interdependent. Therefore I believe that all life is to be honoured and cared for to the best of our abilities.

My 'faith' is about understanding nature's cycles and tides so that I may live in unceasing harmony with them; it is about living sustainably; it is about social justice, environmental justice, economic and political justice for everyone.

My 'faith' calls me to contribute to the communities of which I am a part: my family, the local area where I live and work, my faith community, my wider Interfaith community, my State, Country and communities throughout the world which are linked to each other in so many ways. It is about looking after each other and having compassion for others.

My 'faith' requires that I recognise the divinity within and so aspire to live the best life I can to fulfil the obligations of that divinity. It is about working with the forces of nature – not against them or trying to control them; it is found in studying, understanding, and being constantly amazed by the cycles of life, death and rebirth – realizing that there are times for sowing, tending and harvesting; of waxing and waning, ebbing and flowing, and that this is how life must be because it is unnatural and unsustainable for anything to increase forever. It is about living in harmony with the Wheel of the Year and the flow of the seasons. It is about being the best person I can be in this place, in this time, in the here and now.

Faith is faith, which by definition means that no proof is possible. My thirteen-year-old son has declared that there is no God. I have no means to convince him otherwise. My heart tells me that God exists. Indeed, I have told him quite frankly that I need to believe in God. We have identical sets of facts, but we have chosen to interpret those facts differently. For him, the capriciousness of the world is persuasive evidence that God does not exist. For me, the times in my life that I have felt strengthened and inspired by a presence beyond myself have convinced me that God is very real.

Judaism traditionally has not been so invested in testing the faith of its adherents. Early on following the exile from Israel, the rabbis must have unconsciously realised that the requirement of belief in certain principles was a sure path to divisiveness. Judaism is a non-dogmatic religion, which has given rise to an extraordinary literature of argument and debate. Verses in the Bible which are seen as settled truth by Christians are infinitely open to discussion for Jews.

One of my favourite areas of study is *midrash*, messily translated as rabbinic exegesis. *Midrash* for the rabbis is filling in the holes in the text. Take, for example, Genesis 22, in which God asks Abraham to offer his promised son Isaac as a burnt offering. Why is Abraham tested? Does God act alone, or in dialogue with another? Where is Sarah in the story? How does Isaac feel about it all? Each of these questions has been addressed, and a variety of sometimes mutually-contradictory answers have been recorded. At one stage, an exasperated student asks, "What is the truth?" The answer: "Both these and these are the words of the living God." Judaism has the wonderful tradition of preserving minority views, in the belief that all discussions held for the glory of God are worth keeping. If faith is present in this equation, it is surely found in these debates.

Many of us have seen Sikhs and even worked alongside them without realizing who they are, what they believe, and how they live. We may even have confused them for Arabs or Afghans. We may have wondered about these men who wear colourful turbans over long uncut hair.

Sikhs are not new to Australia. Their first recorded presence dates from 1897, over a hundred years ago; their first place of worship (gurudwara) was established in 1906. The Sikh faith is now one of the five largest faith traditions of the world. There is a significant Sikh community in almost every major city in Australia, with numerous Sikh places of worship and Community Centers. Some of the best banana farmers are Sikh. There is currently a Sikh Councillor in Coffs Harbour. There are Sikh blue collar workers and taxi drivers, Sikh executives and research scientists. Sikhs serve as members of the Armed forces and as members of the Police and the Public Service. Sikhs are also in Health Services and business enterprises.

Compared to other major religions, the Sikh faith is relatively young. Its founder Guru Nanak was born in 1469 in Punjab at a time of great ferment and creative activity in the world – the voyage of Columbus and his discovery of the New World in 1492, the discoveries of Copernicus who was born in 1473, the printing of the Gutenberg Bible in 1462 were among the many remarkable achievements and events of those decades.

To understand his teachings and his disciples, it is necessary to look at Nanak the man and his times.

During Guru Nanak's time in the fifteenth century the two great religious systems of the world – the Vedantic and the traditions of the Old Testament met in Punjab. Fifteenth century India was ruled by Muslims. Indian society of that time was steeped in idol worship, dogma and superstition, and was stratified into castes with rigidly defined duties and rights for each. Neither those of the low castes nor women were allowed to read the Holy Scriptures.

Nanak rejected both the forced conversions by the rulers as well as the caste system, idolatry and the inferior place of women. He taught a message of love. He defined God as gender-free, not woman or man exclusively. He taught of a universal God, common to all mankind – not a Sikh God, a Hindu God, a Moslem God, a Jewish or a Buddhist God, or one limited to any sect, nation, race, creed, color or gender.

Guru Nanak was followed by nine successor-Gurus over two centuries. They further elaborated on his message of universal love and brotherhood – and sisterhood. They made significant contributions to the development of Sikh institutions. Sikhs believe that all ten Gurus represented the spirit of Nanak and spoke with his authority.

Sikhs worldwide celebrated Vaisakhi 1999 as a milestone in Sikh history. It marked 300 years since Guru Gobind Singh decreed the formation of the Khalsa and fashioned the nation of Sikhs.

Guru Gobind Singh also decreed an end to the line of personal Gurus in human form. The writings of the earlier Gurus were collated along with those of Hindu and Moslem saints whose teachings were consistent with Sikh philosophy. This collection – Guru Granth – is thus a uniquely ecumenical and eclectic collection of spiritual writing. For Sikhs Guru Granth is the repository of all spiritual knowledge and authority. In temporal matters all authority rests with the Sikh community worldwide acting democratically and in mindful prayer with an awareness of the spiritual heritage which is embodied in the Guru Granth.

Sikhs revere the ten Gurus – Guru Nanak to Guru Gobind Singh – because they brought to us the divine word but they worship only the one, timeless (Akal) God. For Sikhs the word (shabd) is the eternal Guru. The word "Guru" acquires, therefore, a very special meaning for Sikhs. It is reserved only for the ten Gurus who gave us the divine message and to the shabd contained in the Guru Granth.

The word "Sikh" derivatively means a student. In essence, therefore, a Sikh is and remains a student of the meaning of life.

The Sikh faith tradition is a practical one to be lived here on earth and Sikhs are a pragmatic people. The emphasis is on leading a worldly, successful life as a householder and a contributing member of society but with the mind attuned to an awareness of God, the eternal truth. The Sikh faith rejects all distinctions based on caste, creed, gender, color, race or national origin. God is not found on the mountaintop or by renouncing the world but is found in the life of a householder and in a family.

The philosophic structure of the Sikh faith tradition rests on three equally important legs: an honest living and an honest day's work, sharing with others what God and life have given us, and living life fully – not in half measures – with an awareness of the infinite within each of us.

The Sikh faith enunciates a philosophical concept termed Miri-Piri which means living a worldly life with an active, strong sense of commitment to the world and humanity, governed and directed by a strong foundation and underpinning of spiritual awareness. In a centered existence the internal and external lives are to be integrated. Moral and spiritual values need to form the cornerstone of the successful worldly life. One without the other is incomplete and insufficient.

The Sikh faith tradition is the fifth largest faith tradition in the world. It was founded in the sixteenth century by Guru Nanak in the Punjab district of what is now India and Pakistan. It is based on the teachings of Guru Nanak and the nine Sikh gurus who followed him. Sikhs do not believe in idols and shun the caste system. Sikhs are peaceful people with a strong sense of justice and human rights.

Sikhs believe religion should be practiced by living in the world and coping with life's everyday problems. Sikhs view men and women as being completely equal. Women are expected to participate in daily and religious life in the same way as men.

One does not have to be a Sikh to participate in Sikh religious services and activities. All are welcome to a Sikh Gurdwara or House of the "Guru" which always has its central focus on Guru Granth Sahib 'the Guru Eternal' that is installed and decorated on a throne higher than anyone else in the congregation. In fact, the entire life of a Sikh revolves around Sri Guru Granth Sahib. Women could equally read it, minister it and lead a congregation, no less than men.

In matters that affect the Sikh community, the Sikhs have throughout their history followed a simple but effective mechanism whereby individual voices are heard and decisions reflect the current state of knowledge, information and technology. In all such matters, and in honor of the first five Sikhs who heeded the call of Guru Gobind Singh in 1699, the voice of the community is channeled through five Sikhs, selected and authorized to resolve issues and speak as the voice of the community. Sikhs believe that God and Guru pervade the congregation when these five Sikhs act in mindful prayer. Decision making, thus, becomes a collective process. Sikhs do not have a priestly hierarchy with its associated ecclesiastical authority.

As a faith tradition in which the Word (shabd) is Guru, the Sikh faith values education. Yet it recognizes that the ultimate reality is such that our senses cannot perceive it and our intellect cannot fathom it but our souls can commune with it.

The Sikh faith promises women an equal place. It could do no less when it defines God as gender neutral, and is perhaps one of the few major world religions to do so. Female infanticide, which was not uncommon in India and in much of the world 500 years ago, was strongly condemned by Guru Nanak and his successors. There is no activity in a gurdwara or within the community that is permitted to a man but not to a woman. There is no religious function from which women are barred at any time of their lives.

Sikhs have no food taboos except those that stem from one simple injunction - a life of moderation in which we shun all that harms the body or the mind. Animal sacrifice is forbidden and so is the consumption of animals killed in such manner. This also means that all intoxicants – tobacco, alcohol or any mind altering "recreational" drugs – are forbidden. The Sikh faith teaches that our lives must become a testament to truth and service to mankind.

No matter what their street attire, male Sikhs have been easily recognized by their long unshorn hair covered with a turban. (It needs to be pointed out that in the traditional Indian society only a man of high caste or the ruling class wore a turban.) Sikh women adhere to the same basic life style, symbols, rules and conduct, except that few wear turbans. You might see Sikh boys, who are much too young to handle a turban, walking about in their schools or play grounds with a top-knot of long unshorn hair covered simply with a scarf.

The worship consists of singing of the liturgy as well as exposition of Sikh history, tradition and religion. Non-Sikhs are always welcome. Any layperson – man or woman – may perform any Sikh rites; none are restricted to the ordained clergy.

The Sikh faith tradition (Sikhi) recognizes the universal truths that underlie all human endeavors, religions and belief systems, though people differ in how they institutionalize those beliefs into a code of conduct and a way of life. Much as Sikhs love their faith, the Sikh faith tradition is equally respectful and tolerant of another – a non-Sikh – who loves his or her own religion in his or her own way. Sikhi asks a non-Sikh to discover and live the essential message and meaning of his/her own religion so that a

Christian can become a better Christian, a Jew a better Jew, a Hindu a better Hindu, while a Sikh becomes a better Sikh, and so on.

In 1699 the tenth and last of the Sikh Gurus – Gobind Singh – recognized the growing maturity of his followers in a most dramatic manner. On the day of Vaisakhi (which falls in early to mid-April) 1699, he summoned his followers to a small town (Anandpur) in Punjab. Over 80,000 came. History tells us that Guru Gobind Singh appeared before his people, flashed a naked sword and demanded a head. He repeated his call until five Sikhs volunteered. These five came from different parts of India and from different castes; three were from the so-called lower castes. To these five, and to many others, on that historic April, he bestowed a new discipline, a creed.

The Guru initiated these five in the new order of the Khalsa and then, in a dramatic and historic gesture, they, in turn, initiated him. On that day he gave the Sikhs their modern form which includes five articles of faith:

1) unshorn hair as a gift of God and Guru and a mark of Sikh identity,
2) a small comb for the hair,
3) a steel bracelet which signifies a reality with no beginning and no end, and is also symbolic of a Sikh's commitment to the ideals of his faith, much as wedding ring might indicate fealty and identity,
4) a sword indicative of resolve and commitment to justice, and
5) knee-length breeches in keeping with the disciplined lifestyle of a Sikh.

In Indian society, an individual's name reveals his caste and thus his/her place in society. On Vaisakhi 1699, Guru Gobind Singh freed Sikhs from the caste system by ordaining that all Sikh males incorporate "Singh" meaning a lion and women use "Kaur" meaning a princess into their names, thus shedding their caste identity.

Implied here would be the hope and prayer that a Sikh's life becomes a testament to courage and grace inherent in these names.

I have been involved in the Progressive Christian movement, school, way, for some time now, as well as Celtic pre-Christian spirituality and interfaith dialogue. Within my faith journey I have come to realise that the word 'faith' has many facets. It can stand for an institution, for a blindly-held belief, for trust in some kind of divine pre-destination or protection, and, finally, a broadly held acceptance of something 'beyond' human or mortal parameters.

However there is something else I have come to realise. For me, the word 'faith' stands for mystery, for questioning, even, dare I say it, for doubt! For those of a more traditional, literalist or conservative point of view, that has connotations, and many would see the above epithets as a hindrance to good 'faith'. Traditionalists see progressive theology and overall the progressive faith as being, at the worst, 'wishy-washy', at the best lacking any kind of solid foundation. Recently I heard someone say that we (progressives) are great at pointing out inadequacies and problems, but all we have to put up instead is 'mystery'. Rather than dismiss this out of hand, I have decided to take this on board. A hospital chaplain once told me that when a family comes and asks if their son, about to die, will go to heaven, it is hard to give a 'progressive' answer. Just not what is wanted or needed at that stage, black and white is being sought, certainty. Now for many of us we bask in the UN-certainty, I know I do. The tryst with mystery is what I am all about.

But if there is a 'certainty' to 'faith' it is this, we ebb and flow within a tide of divinity. Whatever the limitless Divine is, it is to this that I am faithful, this I seek to understand and have a transcendental communicative relationship with. This is achieved through prayer, yes, through contemplation and meditation, through intellectual questioning, through taking sacred texts seriously, but not necessarily literally. It is about holding those in authority to account, placing love, and inclusiveness and tolerance as the bench marks that need to be lived up to, it is about engaging in 'faith in action' or acts of social justice, it is about being the template of what you hope the world to be, because for many our actions may be the only Bibles others may ever read and the only 'Church' ever encountered.

Faith, in short, is a verb, not a noun!

Faith is a knowing that divine force first hand. Faith is an acceptance of a higher power. Because God is within us and around us, when we have faith in ourselves, we have faith in God. When we have faith in God we can have faith in others. We can have faith that what we wish for and what we put out into the universe will come to us. We have faith that a Force greater than ourselves connects us and holds a vantage point of all aspects of the universe.

Faith is an interesting concept in Vodou: it implies the need to believe in something without proof, whereas Vodounists have the opportunity to speak with their *lwa* through spirit possession. Most Vodounists therefore would say that faith is not required; rather it is necessary to be prepared for personal relationship with the Divine. Many Vodounists who converted to the religion (rather than be born into it) did so because it is an experiential religion – it offers a direction, a connection to something greater than ourselves, rather than a need to follow the instructions of a parish priest, or similar authority. While there is an *Oungan* or *Manbo* (Priest or Priestess) acting as head of the house, their role is to work as a spiritual guide, aiding each house member in their own spiritual journey and leading them towards a personal relationship with their *lwa*, rather than instructing on dogma or scripture.

When faith is required, it is faith in the community, rather than faith in God; faith that your brothers and sisters in the ounfo will progress on the spiritual journey with you, and support you as you support them.

The idea of faith forms a central part in Theravada Buddhist practice. However, in the earliest texts of the Theravada tradition, written in a language known as 'Pali', the Buddha was critical of blind faith in his teachings and encouraged his followers to test his teachings to see if they worked. In this way, the Buddha approved of a faith that was developed through an experiential validation of his teachings. Therefore, in the Theravada Buddhist tradition, the notion of faith could also be explained equally well by the word 'trust', a faith based on experience.

This trust is central in providing the motivation and energy to continue to practice the Theravada Buddhist path. However, it is often emphasised that, in order to attain liberation, this faith should not develop into an attachment to the religious tradition itself. In the Pali texts, the Buddha compares his teachings to a raft that is meant to be abandoned once it has been used. We should not continue to carry the raft on our shoulders once we have reached the further shore, though it is essential we believe that the raft will carry us across the river, otherwise we would never even set foot on that raft. Faith, then, is an essential component in the Theravada Buddhist path.

This approach to faith as found in the Pali texts does not mean that there is not a place for devotion or worship within the Theravada Buddhist tradition. The so-called 'Three Refuges', the Buddha, his teachings and the Buddhist community, especially the monastic community, are central objects of Theravada worship. Worship often takes the form of offering objects such as incense or flowers to a representation of the Buddha, whether it is an image of him, a text of his teaching or an individual practicing his path. These symbols can also take the form of monastic relics, monuments or pilgrimage sites, for instance. This type of faith, characterised by joyful devotion, is encouraged within the Theravada tradition as it is often considered to create beneficial mental states. For instance, the calm or joy of making an offering to the Buddha, his teachings or Buddhist community can provide the basis for further mental culture and can remove the unhelpful mental states that might hinder Buddhist practice.

Therefore, within the Theravada Buddhist tradition, faith is important as it can take the form of trust in the teachings of the Buddha, created through the experience of testing and practicing his teachings. In addition, a more devotional faith is recognised as being beneficial for creating a joyful and calm mind that can remove the unhelpful mental states that are obstacles on the Buddhist path. However, it cannot be ignored that a central component of the Theravada Buddhist path is the practice of letting go of the tendency to identify with objects of desire as 'I' or 'mine', since they are subject to change and do not have the permanence we unconsciously ascribe to them. Their inevitable change and end is a reality that ruptures our unconscious desire for their permanence. This desire is attachment and this rupture causes suffering. In this way, the Buddha recognised that his path too could be an object of attachment and therefore encouraged his followers to be wary of blind faith.

Faith is the state of mind and soul which enables you to put your trust in something bigger than yourself. It is a force outside of your control. It is a desire to connect with that which cannot be seen, touched, smelt or heard. Even though Faith is intangible it holds us, enabling us to engage with the world around us in a positive proactive way.

Is Faith the inability to be choose for oneself, a desire to rely on someone/thing else rather than yourself? No, faith in God is the rudder which guides my journey, the knowledge that I don't have to take it alone and that even at my most desperate hour I will be carried. It is not a crutch for, at times, it challenges rather than supports, – it is not always easy to do the right thing, but the knowledge that you are required to live by a certain code lightens the load – giving structure to what is often a very unstructured world.

Islam teaches us that there is a whole network of support out there if we choose to take it.

As Muslims we believe in the articles of Faith:

One God;

The angels of God; who have a variety of tasks including watching over us;

The books of God, especially the Qur'an; (the People of the Book are the Jews and Christians and therefore the Torah and the Bible are part of this article, this gives us a wealth of teachings and traditions to draw on in our daily lives);

The prophets of God (peace be upon them all), especially Mohammed (peace be upon him); (including Adam, Abraham, Noah, Moses, and Jesus, just to name a few);

The Day of Judgment (or the afterlife); and

The supremacy of God's will (this does not mean that Muslims do not have free will but that our faith teaches us that if God is all of the things we profess him to be then He must have our best interests at heart. If you believe this with all that you are then you will submit yourself to his plan rather than your own. But how do you know what His plan really is...it's simply a matter of Faith!)

Contrary to some opinions, faith is the exact opposite of 'what you believe in.' Often religious (especially conservative Christian) people state that faith is complete trust, certainty, absolute assurance etc. In my past I've been part of Church communities where faith is viewed in a quasi magical way – i.e. that it has its own power to actually force God to work on your behalf. There was a whole phase (back in the 80s) of 'name it and claim it' Christianity where one exercised 'faith' by stating what you wanted (be it health, wealth or whatever) and, rather than wait for the miracle to emerge, actually act as if you already have it. The (dubious) theory behind it is far too detailed to explain here but it's all to do with an obscure Old Testament text with regard to the covenant God (Yahweh) made with Abraham and his descendants, and the notion that modern day born-again Christians are his spiritual descendents – thus they can name and claim the promised gifts given to him all those thousands of years ago (promises of prosperity and health etc.). Thus modern Christians can name and claim what they want 'to live like true children of the King, princes and princesses.' *Bollocks!*

In this context I've seen people throw away their medication as an act of such 'faith' and watched them descend into the hell of depression and psychosis.

I have to say that, though this idea comes from an extremely different tradition, it does seem to have certain links (at least in the sort of practises that can emerge from it) to the most literalistic end of the modern day 'Law of Attraction' theory. I'm sure that there is truth somewhere in this, and positive living is crucial for a happy life, *but* I doubt whether it actually happens in such an automatic way as many seem to express. I think there's a huge difference in faith that teaches you 'have what you want' and faith that teaches you how to 'want what you have.' The latter is not only more realistic but makes for a happier and more grounded life (especially for those of us who will never live in a Californian mansion).

So my answer to the question 'what is faith' is simply this. Faith is the ability to live with doubt, uncertainty, mess, muddle and occasional broken dreams YET with a deep down inner peace that allow you to let go and allow the will of the universe to unfold for your essential goodness – whatever journey it happens to lead you on.

CHAPTER THREE

What is 'Evil'?

Evil is the desire within ourselves to push our own agenda, to come out on top regardless of how you get there.. Evil belittles, denies and corrupts, leaving its victim empty and afraid. This fear is often fed by more fear and emptiness thus creating a viscous cycle that the individual cannot or will not recognise and stop. Those consumed by evil are unable, or unwilling, to see their fragility and are therefore incapable of identifying it in others.

Evil invades ourdeep feelings of inadequacy making us also unable to accept those same flaws in others. It is the disconnect between ourselves and other human beings. The desire to be right no matter what the cost or to have our way despite the damage we may cause.

Most of all, evil is fear in action.

Evil convinces those who are consumed by self doubt, anger, failure or disappointment that to make others pay for their misery or unhappiness is acceptable and at times even admirable.

Evil seduces and then destroys all who come into contact with it.

Often evil will be so well disguised we recognise it as our friend. It can lead us to believe that we are better than others and so therefore deserve more; more love, friends, things, power, recognition. There is nothing wrong in wanting to attain these things but. if consumed by them, this journey once achieved can be a lonely one.

Evil feeds well into our human desire for self preservation and at times this desire evolves into the disregard at best, oppression at worst, of others' beliefs, cultures, opinions and dreams. For it to exist we need to be open to its ability to dehumanise others and accept this as an acceptable position to take.

"If you are not careful, the newspapers will have you hating the people who are being oppressed, and loving the people who are doing the oppressing".
Malcolm X (Muslim American Civil Rights Activist)

This is a question that I am not fully ready to answer. Evil clearly exists. Just one glance at any daily newspaper will give enough examples of evil things that occur – from the teenager who's stabbed in a racist street attack to the billionaire businessman who wants more and more and more, to the bishop who allows vile priestly perversions to simply be moved to another parish. Surely one cannot deny that evil exists – but is it an inner psychological force or an outer spiritual force, or both? This is what I do not yet feel qualified to answer.

I feel that, within humanity, evil is most likely to be part of our own repressed 'shadow' that, in some, can get out of control. I guess I know there are times when I find myself projecting 'stuff' out there onto others. Usually people I find hard to bare (if I'm honest and if I really look hard) remind me of things about myself I do not like. This is classic projection and I feel it's what individuals, communities, cultures, whole countries and even religions can do. We can create enemies over 'there' so we do not have to face them and deal with them 'over here.'

But is that the whole story? Is it purely psychological? Are there actual entities or presences 'out there' that would infiltrate and seek to overpower humans? Is possession real? Back in theological college I would have said 'of course not, we're far too clever and educated now to believe in all that demonic nonsense.' But now? Well now I'm not so sure. I need to think some more about this whole question.

The rabbis have an elegant, if not always satisfying answer for the existence of evil: they adhere to a concept of God who has granted free will to human beings. It is up to us to choose what kind of lives we will lead — good or evil, positive or negative. Our religion believes fiercely in the concept of repentance. Each of us, through sheer force of will and with the help of God, can free ourselves from our worst attributes. The medieval rabbi Moses ben Maimon in his masterly work 'The Laws of Repentance' spells out a detailed procedure that may be followed by even the most heinous sinner to become a better person. For those guilty of particularly terrible actions, Rabbi Moses recommends taking on a new name to represent a break with the past. Logically, if free will does not exist, repentance is meaningless.

Nevertheless, the existence of evil represents a significant challenge of faith, primarily because its consequences are allowed to unfold without any divine interference. Years ago, a young student asked me, "If God could part the Red Sea, why couldn't God stop the Holocaust?" It is a question I am still asked by those in my congregation who lived through that most horrifying time and are tortured by their memories. Where was God? Is there no evil so terrible that it will trigger a response from the divine?

The question of evil is also significant for Jews because we have suffered disproportionately simply for being who we are. An old joke exclaims, "If this is what it means to be chosen, perhaps God could choose someone else!" Too often, our persecutors have believed they were acting in the name of faith and good, and good and righteous people suffered as a result.

I am a realist: if God were to descend from heaven, God would have done so in World War II and in the midst of the many genocides that have come since then. This is not going to happen. It is up to us. When I am asked what we can learn from the horror of the Holocaust, my response is to call upon Jews and all other caring human beings to fight injustice and genocide whenever and wherever it might arise. If we do so, our hands and hearts will truly be doing God's work.

This is another concept where the Celtic Pagan world-view differs from that of others. The monotheistic faiths have a fundamental belief in oppositional dualities – good and evil, right and wrong, man and woman, body and spirit – a world of black and white. The Celtic world-view is one of complimentary dualities where each half is necessary to create a complete being. God and Goddess together constitute the Divine, male and female attributes together make a human animal, the physical and the spiritual together form a sentient being, the seeds of creation and destruction are found in each other. Using an image of a monochrome world, the Celtic world is made up of myriad shades of grey, from the palest silver-white to the deepest grey-black and everything in between.

The four elements are a wonderful example of this complementary duality. The Earth is our Mother, providing food to give us life and shelter for comfort and security; but an earthquake or volcano can leave us exposed to nature's fury and bereft of sustenance. We need air to breathe to survive on this planet, and gentle breezes cool us in the heat of summer – yet the force of a cyclone destroys all in its path and a storm at sea can sink the greatest ship. We need water for our bodies to survive, we are in fact 70% water, but we can also drown in it and too much can poison our systems. Fire allows us to cook our food and keep warm, it enables certain seeds to germinate – but it also burns and destroys. We also note that after each cycle of destruction there is an awe-inspiring rebirth and re-creation of life. So, within each element are the seeds of life and death, creation and destruction – for each element manifests the cycle of life, death and rebirth which is central to Celtic Pagan belief.

Because the Celtic world-view is grounded in the belief in complementary dualities, there is no all-powerful force for good and there is no opposing all-powerful force embodying evil. Celtic deity is understood as the soul or spirit that animates all elements of the natural world: it is neither 'good' nor 'evil' – it just 'is'. Evil, therefore, is not found in nature. Volcanic eruptions, tsunami, earthquakes, floods, bushfires – none of these are evil in and of themselves. Natural disasters are just that – part of the natural cycles of the earth, with no sentient intention to harm. As devastating as these natural disasters are, in the Celtic perspective they are not seen as the punishments of an angry God brought about by the 'sins' of His creations, or the workings of a malevolent incarnation of evil aiming to destroy man's faith in an all-knowing, all-seeing and all-powerful Creator, and tempting him to break the rules imposed by that Creator. Natural disasters just 'are'.

Similarly, non-human animals act and react to the laws of nature – carnivores hunt to survive, and kill only what they need to feed themselves and their families. Males fight, not for pleasure, but so that the strongest will reproduce ensuring the continuance of the group. Nature can be incredibly harsh; survival can be a continual struggle; but non-human animals work in harmony with the cycles of nature and live sustainably. Again, in the Celtic Pagan world-view their behaviour is not regarded as either good or evil – their actions are part of the cycle of life, death and rebirth; they are an integral part of the interconnected web of all living things.

So, if 'evil' exists it has emerged through the actions of humans as they have evolved and moved from their original position in the natural world. As community groups and societies developed, leaders emerged and formulated the rules that would govern the behaviour of members of the group. Some groups said their laws came from God, some were made up by men. Throughout the world there are as many different laws by which people live as there are ecosystems on the planet. The majority of these laws are determined by the cultural, historical, religious and geographical bases of the communities they govern, which is why there is such a diversity of understanding of what constitutes 'good' and 'evil'. Whatever the understanding, however, a common element of all laws is that they are a social construct used by leaders to control the behaviour of the rest of the community so society can function smoothly. Thus, a 'good' citizen is one who obeys the laws and a 'bad' citizen is one who breaks the laws.

Ultimately, 'evil' is a human judgement and ever changeable. Today what Western society views as 'evil' (unethical and immoral in today's terminology) was only a few hundred years ago the ruling morality – slavery, child labour, dispossession of people from their land, the alienation of physically and mentally disabled people, the persecution of women, Jews, Moslems, gypsies, homosexuals, non-Caucasians and indigenous people of every colonised continent.

The word 'sin', which many faiths equate with the word 'evil', comes originally from the Hebrew *khate* and Greek *harmatia* – and both have the meaning of 'missing the mark'. From a Celtic Pagan perspective, this is a very apt definition because it explains the notion that 'evil' is behaviour or intention that is not in harmony with the society in which you live. Such intentions and their enactment 'miss the mark' of acceptable behaviour – bringing shame and dishonour to both the perpetrator and their family, and leading in extreme cases to exile from the clan group. For individual honour – the social perception of a person's level of truthfulness, right action (generosity and service) and loyalty – is central to the standing of a person in the Celtic Pagan world-view. It is from this perspective that 'good' and 'evil' actions are defined. To behave in a dishonourable way, or with dishonourable intent, shows that a person is disconnected from the web of life; is disassociated from the cycles of nature and the interrelationship of each and every soul present within the web. Honour also requires a person to take full responsibility for their actions and their consequences – both intended and accidental.

As a Celtic Pagan I cannot say "The Devil made me do it", there is no scapegoat to drive into the wilderness – there is only personal accountability for the choices made and their consequences. To live honourably is to accept responsibility for what we do, or fail to do, and to make restitution for any harm caused by our actions. In a Celtic Pagan world 'evil' can be seen as the denial of that responsibility, which in turn causes ripples of disharmony throughout the interconnected web of life affecting everything in the natural world.

According to the Bahá'í teachings of the oneness of God, there can be no such thing as positive evil. There can only be one Infinite. If there were any other power in the universe outside of or opposed to the One, then the One would not be infinite. Just as darkness is but the absence or lesser degree of light, so evil is but the absence or lesser degree of good.[25]

The Bahá'í teachings state:

"In creation there is no evil, all is good. Certain qualities and natures innate in some men and apparently blameworthy are not so in reality. For example, from the beginning of his life you can see in a nursing child the signs of greed, of anger and of temper. Then, it may be said, good and evil are innate in the reality of man, and this is contrary to the pure goodness of nature and creation. The answer to this is that greed, which is to ask for something more, is a praiseworthy quality provided that it is used suitably. So, if a man is greedy to acquire science and knowledge, or to become compassionate, generous and just, it is most praiseworthy. If he exercises his anger and wrath against the bloodthirsty tyrants who are like ferocious beasts, it is very praiseworthy; but if he does not use these qualities in a right way, they are blameworthy... It is the same with all the natural qualities of man, which constitute the capital of life; if they be used and displayed in an unlawful way, they become blameworthy. Therefore, it is clear that creation is purely good."[26]

The Bahá'í Faith does not therefore accept the concept of 'original sin' or any related doctrine which considers that people are basically evil or have intrinsically evil elements in their nature. All the forces and faculties within us are God-given and thus potentially beneficial to our spiritual development. If a person, through his own God-given free will, turns away from this force or fails to make the necessary effort to develop his spiritual capacities, the result is imperfection. In this sense it can be said that *"evil is imperfection."*[27] Such imperfections occur both within the individual and in society. It is in struggling against these imperfections that we develop the spiritual capacities which are our birthright.

If a tiger kills and eats another animal, this is not evil, because it is an expression of the tiger's natural instinct for survival. But if a person kills and eats a fellow human being, this same act may be considered evil because man is capable of doing otherwise. Such an act is not an expression of his true nature.

According to the Bahá'í teachings, humans have both a material nature, such as the animal instincts of the tiger, and a higher spiritual nature, which includes the rational mind, the soul and conscience. The development of our highest potential involves controlling our material side as we develop our spiritual side – as it is only the spiritual that endures.

God has created us with free will, and we can choose to act against the interests of our true nature and to develop unhealthy appetites. We all have certain intrinsic needs that demand satisfaction. These needs are partly physical (tangible) and partly spiritual (intangible). God has provided for the legitimate satisfaction of all our needs. The teachings of the Manifestations provide loving guidance on how to satisfy them in a healthy way. But if, whether through simple ignorance or wilful rebellion, we try to satisfy some of our needs in an illegitimate or unhealthy way, then we may distort our true nature and generate within ourselves new appetites incapable of genuine satisfaction:

"... capacity is of two kinds: natural capacity and acquired capacity. The first, which is the creation of God, is purely good – in the creation of God there is no evil; but the acquired capacity has become the cause of the appearance of evil. For example, God has created all men in such a manner and has given them such a constitution and such capacities that they are benefited by sugar and honey and harmed and destroyed by poison. This nature and constitution is innate, and God has given it equally to all mankind. But man begins little by little to accustom himself to poison by taking a small quantity each day, and gradually increasing it, until he reaches such a point that he cannot live without a gram of opium every day. The natural capacities are thus completely perverted. Observe how much the natural capacity and constitution can be changed, until by different habits and training they become entirely perverted. One does not criticize vicious people because of their innate capacities and nature, but rather for their acquired capacities and nature."[28]

Bahá'u'lláh said that pride, or self-centeredness, is one of the greatest hindrances to spiritual progress. Pride represents an exaggerated sense of one's own importance in the universe and leads to an attitude of superiority over others. The prideful person feels as though he is or ought to be in absolute control of his life and the circumstances surrounding it, and he seeks power and dominance over others because such power helps him maintain this illusion of superiority. Thus, pride is a hindrance to spiritual growth because it impels the prideful individual on an endless quest to fulfil the expectations of his vainly-conceived and illusory self-concept.

In other words, the key to understanding Bahá'í morality and ethics is to be found in the Bahá'í notion of spiritual progress: that which is conducive to spiritual progress is good, and whatever tends to hinder spiritual progress is bad. Thus, from the

Bahá'í viewpoint, learning 'good' from 'bad' (or 'right' from 'wrong') means attaining a degree of self-knowledge that permits us to know when something is helpful to our spiritual growth and when it is not. And this knowledge can only be obtained through the teachings of the Manifestations.

Bahá'u'lláh repeatedly stressed that only revealed religion can save us from our imperfections. It is because God has sent his Manifestations to show us the path to spiritual development and to touch our hearts with the spirit of God's love that we are able to realize our true potential and make the effort to be united with God. This is the 'salvation' that religion brings. It does not save us from the stain of some 'original sin', nor does it protect us from some external evil force or devil. Rather, it delivers us from captivity to our own lower nature, a captivity that breeds private despair and threatens social destruction, and it shows us the path to a deep and satisfying happiness.

Indeed, the essential reason for such widespread unhappiness and terrible social conflict and crises in the world today is that humankind has turned away from true religion and spiritual principles. The only salvation in any age, Bahá'ís believe, is to turn again towards God, to accept his Manifestation for that day, and to follow his teachings.[29]

The Theravada Buddhist understanding of evil differs from its conception in other religious traditions. This contrast has its basis in the markedly different approach to the mechanism by which we face the consequences of our actions. In many monotheistic traditions the moral consequences of our actions are judged by God and justice is mediated by God. However, as I have shown above, Theravada Buddhist practice does not necessitate the existence of God. The goal of Theravada Buddhism, *nirvana*, is primarily characterised as the end of suffering and the Theravada path is conducive to the end of suffering. Therefore, the Buddha often divides our actions by those which aid the attainment of *nirvana* and those that do not. Those actions that end greed, hatred and delusion, the primary causes of our suffering, are seen as skilful actions and can be interpreted as being 'good'. Those unskilful actions that only help fuel the fires of greed, hatred and delusion can be considered 'bad' or 'evil'.

According to the tradition, evil actions lead us to suffer automatically because they support the characteristics that cause us to suffer. Likewise, good actions lead us to suffer less since they remove the characteristics that cause us to suffer. This is the basic principle of the law of *karma*, an independent moral mechanism that does not require a divine principle. Within the Theravada Buddhist tradition, the root of greed, hatred and delusion is a belief in the independent existence of 'I', our identification with our own egos. Therefore, an even more distilled explanation of the law of *karma* is that any action that fuels our identification with our ego is evil and leads to suffering and any action that lessens our identification with our ego is good and leads to less suffering. Evil, then, in Theravada Buddhism is characterised by any action that leads one away from the attainment of *nirvana*.

Within the Theravada Buddhist tradition, this understanding of evil is often personified as a figure known as 'Mara'. In Theravada literature, Mara is often represented as a being who attempts to lead a practitioner away from the Buddhist path and towards actions not conducive to the attainment of *nirvana*. However, it is important to note that the scholastic tradition of Theravada Buddhism recognises that the figure of 'Mara' simultaneously represents a psychological state of ignorance, which is marked by the three fires of existence, viz. greed, hatred and delusion, and a belief in a permanent, independent self.

While Vodou recognises God as a creator figure, there is no evil counterpart like Satan. Evil therefore is not embodied in any particular figure, and that makes it a fluid concept based on perspective. Given Vodou's close relationship with the Slave Trade and slave conditions in the New World colonies, there are some core practices that could be considered evil. These would centre on the removal of another person's free will, or rights, which would equate to making them a slave.

Beyond that, evil is difficult to define. There are certainly acts that are considered 'bad', such as murder, rape, theft and so forth, but these are acts against society, not God, and so defining them as 'evil' is problematic. The God of Vodou is simply a creator, and has no interaction or even interest in the affairs of humanity; therefore laws defining good and bad behaviour are based on human morals, not the word of God.

The 'moral compass' of Vodou is each individual's *ti-bon-ange*, the divine spark that connects each person to the cosmic Divinity. The *ti-bon-ange* acts as a conscience, and tries to point each person to the notion of truth and goodness as the highest path. Each person is free to act on their own, however, and as there is no 'Hell', each individual is answerable only to the community in which they live. The community will respond according to the action.

It is not unheard of, in Haiti, for one person to visit a *Bokor*, or sorcerer, to buy a curse to put on another person. Even though the curse may be aimed at sickness, loss of crops and income, or even death, this is not necessarily considered 'evil'. If someone believes they are cursed, it is likely that they would contact their *Oungan* or *Manbo*, who will be schooled in how to counteract the curse. In some cases, the cursed person may even visit the same *Bokor* to have a curse placed on the person who cursed them. None of these actions could really be considered evil, though the community may condemn the person for trying to curse a member of their community.

A person may even take part in activities that are bad for the community, and claim it is at the request of the *lwa*. The *lwa* are not Gods, and they are subject to the same petty influences as humans, so it is possible that a *lwa* may direct a follower to take action against another person. Generally, however, the *lwa* aim to guide and support their communities, so if such a claim was made, it would likely be investigated by the local *Oungan* or *Manbo*.

Evil is misdirected force; an energy or action out of balance with Divine Will. When we become so imbalanced within ourselves and the Universe in which we have presence, we align with perspectives harmful to ourselves and others. Good, bad, black and white, negative and positive, yin and yang, are all aspects of balance within this world we inhabit. We live within the confines of these principles and evil is just another aspect of these principles.

Definitions of evil vary, however actions commonly considered evil include: conscious and deliberate wrongdoing, discrimination designed to harm others, humiliation of people designed to diminish their psychological needs and dignity, destructiveness, and acts of unnecessary and indiscriminate violence that are not legitimate acts of self-defense but aggressive and designed to cause harm to others.

Evil is the absence of good. Faith traditions have a great deal to say about 'good' and 'evil'. All religions teach the difference between good and evil, but have different beliefs about evil and suffering. Religious leaders and sacred texts all encourage believers to live 'good' lives. The problem of evil and suffering is one of the commonest reasons people give for not believing in God.

There are two types of evil. Natural evil is suffering caused by events that have nothing to do with humans, and which are to do with the way the world is, for example, natural disasters such as volcanic eruptions, floods or earthquakes. Moral (or human) evil is suffering caused by humans acting in a way that is considered morally wrong e.g., bullying, murder, rape, theft or terrorism.

Human evil and natural evil can often work together, with human evil making natural evil worse – or better! For example, the suffering caused by an earthquake or floods can be made worse by people looting, but it can be made more bearable by people showing compassion and making personal sacrifices to help those who are suffering. It is important to remember that: 'evil' is a cause of suffering; 'suffering' is a result of evil.

Sikhs believe Truth is the highest virtue but higher still is truthful living. As such they try to avoid all forms of evil and devote their lives to selfless service to others – *sewa*.

From the time of Guru Nanak five hundred years ago until today, Sikh places of worship (*gurdwaras*) all over the world run free community kitchens, which provide meals to the needy. These kitchens are manned and funded by volunteers. Since in the traditional Indian society people of high and low caste would not mix, nor would they break bread together, the community kitchen (*langar*) of the Sikhs serves to teach the concept of equality by shattering all barriers of caste and class.

The Sikh place of worship (*gurdwara*) is more than that – a place of worship. It has historically served as a refuge for the homeless, the helpless and the destitute. Gurdwaras usually display and fly the 'Nishan Sahib', a yellow (saffron) triangular flag bearing the Sikh symbol of 'Khanda'. Visitors, irrespective of their religion are offered shelter, comfort and food. The only conditions being that they remove the shoes and cover the head. In a gurdwara no special place or seat may be reserved or set aside for any dignitary.

Human dignity and justice form a cornerstone of Sikh teaching, Sikh history speaks of tremendous sacrifice in the cause of freedom and justice. Two Sikh Gurus – the fifth Guru Arjan and the ninth Guru Tegh Bahadur were martyrs to the cause of freedom of religion. The tenth Nanak – Guru Gobind Singh – fought several battles and saw his sons die in battle.

Buddhism does not posit evil as an external force or that any being is intrinsically evil. Uncomfortable with the absolutist connotations that come with the word, Mahāyāna eschews 'evil' for *unskilful* or *unwholesome* thoughts and actions. These are defined as impure mental, verbal and bodily actions that harm others and ourselves, whether obviously or subtly. Historically, Buddhism has based its lay precepts (that is, the series of vows to abstain from) upon what ancient Indian society has seen as 'evil' and disruptive to social order: taking life, theft, sexual misconduct, lying and intoxicants. All Buddhist traditions also share the concept of the Five Grave Offences (*anantarika-karma*): patricide, matricide, murder of an *arhat* (saint), and spilling the blood of a Buddha, or causing disharmony/dissension/schism within a religious community. These really involve external phenomena and are actually manifestations of what all traditions see as the true source of evil (and good): the mind.

For all Buddhist traditions, the battleground has never been between 'good' and 'evil' (since this presumes that there is only one side to empathise with!), but between the causes of suffering and that which releases sentient beings from suffering. Perhaps in a poetic sense, it is *suffering* that Buddhism sees as 'evil' since it is this alone that is worthy of eradication – the historical Buddha spent forty-five years preaching a path that led to the cessation of suffering. A crucial point in the Mahāyāna is that Buddhas, as the supreme beings, don't wish to see beings suffer and will do everything to remove that suffering.

But what are these aforementioned causes? Buddhism proposes the root to be craving – for objects of the senses, for existence, for non-existence (of oneself, one's circumstances or others), for permanence in a fundamentally impermanent world (which is intimately tied with ignorance). A scholar has summed up this position briefly: "Thus it is not the objects of sense desire that cause us suffering, but our attachment to those; it is not views, precepts and vows, and the doctrine of self that in themselves cause suffering but our attachment."[30] And of course, not all attachments are equal. While a rigid, legalistic attachment to the precept of not taking life can be a headache to others, it is of course preferable to a craving to justify bad deeds in the name of religion.

Mahāyāna psychology highlights the suffering caused by thought patterns that manifest when one strays from moderation (the famous Buddhist Middle Way). These extremities entail the physical extremes of self-destruction and sense-indulgence, but even more dangerous are the extreme views of dogmatism or attachments to views. The Mahāyāna warns against that these inner extremes plant the mental seeds delusion, arrogance, and close-mindedness. They plant the excuses for wars and crusades, and justify or condone violence, rape and the physical destruction of civilizations. And for that Mahāyāna sees this subtle, sometimes understandable, even innocent attachment or craving to any ideal – even if they seem noble – as leading to the greatest suffering and evil of all.

We are all capable of evil, just as we are of good. This does not establish a moral duality, however. In the Pagan traditions there is neither an absolute embodied force for either good or evil; the cosmos does not war with itself. Our celebration and reverence of Life encompasses all of Life in every aspect. We respect and honour the darkness, as well as the light, as the sun makes his voyage across the sky. Night and day may seem to provide us with an example of natural opposition; however the emphasis is not on the duality and therefore not on any 'moralising' of these elemental realms.

Phyllis Curott, an eminent Wiccan activist and high priestess from the States, once defined evil as that state which arises when humanity is disconnected from Nature. I agree with this completely. I must qualify this statement by adding that both the concept of 'Nature' as both reality and principle does not simply mean the 'green' or the surrounding environment composed of rivers, trees, rocks and dirt; Nature is All that Is. Nature, to quote Spinoza, is God and God is Nature. To flow with the Pure Will of one's Nature is to therefore enter one's destined orbit – the pathway that unfolds organically from the soul's journey when it becomes conscious of itself and aligns to what I call Own Holy Self. The only ethic I merit is the one that states that total freedom equals total responsibility. First and foremost, *I* am responsible for *my own* actions, thoughts and deeds. To align with my personal Ethos which is an extension of my Pure Will and the core values I hold to be irrevocably sacred (and to which I must attempt to remain congruent) is to enter into a sacred contract whereby I ignite my awareness and embrace my personal responsibility. Thus I become Sovereign of Self. As the Dalai Lama once said – world peace begins with inner peace.

Evil is to consciously cultivate a character of hypocrisy; to desecrate one's Pure Will and to dishonour Nature. One person is not made evil by one act of malevolence or ill-intent; however, if one decided to choose this intent continuously and with relish, then one's Ethos (which means 'character') could be determined as evil.

In reference to the greater sphere of contemporary Paganisms, the concept of evil as a moral absolute opposing the pure embodiment of the force of good is one which does not hold water. To quote Kresphontes, a Hellenic Pagan:

"No dualism of good and evil exists in the Immortal Cosmos. We become virtuous only because we choose to be such."

I agree entirely with this wisdom teaching. I am good because I choose to do good things because it is good to do so, not because

I am advertising a hellish fate or focussing on repressing evil.

Pagans tend not to pay heed to what some of the Abrahamic sectarians obsess over as 'evil'. We are not moralisers intent on bringing all to conformity with some perceived monolithic will; we are ethicists intent on empowering each and every being to touch the core of the Divine within.

The inspirational priest and scholar Matthew Fox once quoted Eckhart when he said, "You may call God love; you may call God goodness; but the best name for God is Compassion."[31] It was Fox's incredible work 'Original Blessings' which first pointed me towards the notion that the fall/redemption theology of the Church was one that was counter-productive to a true embracing of humanity and divinity being bound in joyous 'good'. The notion that we come into this world with 'original sin' was, to Fox, abhorrent, and I echo those sentiments. We are born, instead, into blessing, compassion, and love, though sometimes the world and/or humanity can take that blessing, compassion and love away very rapidly.

It would be useless to argue that there is no such thing as 'evil' in the world, and by that I mean 'NOT'. Not God, not love, not good, not compassion, not being all we can be. And, sadly, this 'not' is everywhere. And because it seems so incongruous to Christians that this can somehow have been a part of God's 'plan', a huge duality of God and the Devil was created to explain the existence of evil and suffering. This makes perfect sense, instead of dealing with complex theological notions of why bad things happen, it is much easier to blame the 'evil one'.

But there are a lot of notions predicating this. The first is the notion that there is indeed some kind of reward and punishment in the afterlife akin to heaven and hell. Another notion is that God is like a puppeteer, interfering in our life on a daily basis, and if something goes awry, this must be because another evil puppeteer has taken over. And finally there is a notion that we as human beings are not 'meant' to suffer or experience evil, that if we had stayed in Eden we would be living some kind of Utopian existence with paradise in every corner. The Church's concepts of evil are predicated on the notion that humanity can only take responsibility for it, or even conquer it, by not 'sinning'. Sadly, those notions have led to a list of actions and beliefs considered to be 'sinful', a list created through social mores, political expediency and, let's face it, old fashioned bigotry.

Instead of a fall/redemption theology, I embrace the notion that 'evil' is often caused by injustice and a lack of balance in the standard of living in the world, though, I admit, not always. There are and will always be psychopaths, of course, but much hatred and abandonment of moral decision-making can surely be stopped if all in this world are treated, by us, by humanity, as we ourselves would wish to be treated. It may sound trite, but the Golden Rule is present in almost every faith, yet so easily ignored. Rather than attribute 'evil' to an external evil super-power akin to God, or to 'sinful' behaviour, let us attribute it to we, as people, not doing what we can for others.

If evil is 'not' then by not ensuring equality, tolerance, inclusiveness, parity and fairness for all, aren't we engaging in acts of evil?

CHAPTER FOUR

What is Contemplation?

Contemplation in Theravada Buddhism is largely encapsulated by the practice of meditation. There are a variety of different meditation practices within the Theravada Buddhist tradition and also many objects of meditation. However, here, I will outline the basic details of meditation and its relationship to the Theravada Buddhist path.

Within the Theravada tradition, meditation is generally divided into two separate practices, concentration and insight. The goal of concentration meditation is to focus the mind on a single object and to calm and refine the mind by not being distracted by any other object than the one being focused on. A common meditation object, for instance, is the breath. When using the breath as an object of concentration meditation, a meditator often focuses on the sensation of breathing in and breathing out. This is often done by directing the mind towards the rising and falling of the stomach or by focusing on the breath entering and leaving the nose. By focusing our attention on this object, our mind begins to calm and our thoughts and agitations lessen. It is as if a glass of dirty water, when made turbid by being shaken, is left still in one place and settles into clarity.

This type of concentration, if practiced regularly, can produce extremely subtle and refined mental states, inaccessible to the untrained mind. However, the goal of concentration meditation is not these exalted states. They are merely by-products. The aim of concentration meditation is to calm the mind in preparation for insight meditation. Within the Theravada Buddhist tradition, insight meditation generally involves taking the "Three Marks" of our existence as objects of contemplation. These three marks represent the fact that our existence is 1) unsatisfactory, 2) impermanent and 3) not independent. This type of contemplation may involve discursive thinking but often simply means resting our concentrated mind on a facet of one of these three principles. For instance, by observing in meditation the fluctuation of our feelings and thoughts we can contemplate the impermanence of existence.

By developing insights on the unsatisfactory, impermanent and dependent nature of existence, the meditator begins to let go of their attachments to their own ego and the objects around them. In doing so, the three fires of greed, hatred and delusion are quenched and we begin to suffer less. Ultimately, we relinquish our incessant desire to control and let-go of all ideas of permanence completely. We understand that our sense of independent identity is grounded in the ego and therefore we no longer identify with the ego. In addition, as a result of no longer identifying with the ego, we no longer identify the objects of our desire as 'mine'. This 'letting-go' does not mean that we get rid of all the objects of our desire. In fact everything remains as it was, nothing is removed. It is only our relationship with our sense of 'I' and the objects of our existence that changes. Complete 'letting go' or *nirvana* does not lie in experience itself but in our relationship to experience. It is by changing our relationship to experience, not experience itself, that we can end suffering forever.

Vodou is an experiential religion, rather than a contemplative religion. While practices such as yoga and meditation are often incorporated into contemporary urban Vodou, there is little that would smoothly equate to Christian concepts of prayer and contemplation. Instead, Vodounists take part in ceremonies and rituals that engage the community as well as the *lwa*, or spirits.

Ceremonies take place regularly; for some groups, this means weekly or even every few days, and for others it means less often, but certainly on significant festival days or times of cultural significance. Traditionally, a ceremony will focus on making an offering or sacrifice to a particular *lwa*, or group of *lwa*, and then spending time with that *lwa* once the offering has been accepted.

The ceremony is usually accompanied throughout by drumming and, at times, other musical accompaniment. The drumming tends to comprise complex polyrhythmic patterns that, along with sustained dancing, help the Vodounists enter an altered or higher state of consciousness. The *Oungan* or *Manbo* will lead the ceremony, and a number of other members of the house will take on supporting roles. Many songs are sung throughout the ceremony in a 'call and response' style. Different *lwa* prefer different songs and dances, so the specific nature of each ceremony depends on the *lwa* being called.

Ceremonies begin fairly formally, with particular litanies being offered to the *lwa*, and the relevant veves (complex symbols connected to each *lwa*) being drawn on the ground to attract the spirits. Intricate dance steps are performed, and offerings are placed around the centre pole within the peristyle. If there is an animal to be sacrificed (which is common in Haiti and some Diaspora groups, though less so in urban American Houses) then the sacrifice takes place at this point, again using a number of specific steps to highlight the significance of the sacrifice. (In Haiti, one of the poorest countries in the Western Hemisphere, the enormity of sacrificing a goat or pig, which may be the family's most valuable asset, cannot be understated. It is therefore carried out with appropriate gravity, and afterwards, the meat of the animal is used to feed the community).

Following the slaughter of the animal and the offering of the other gifts, the formality gives way to a free and increasingly frenetic dance, during which time the *lwa* will appear, possessing one of the more experienced Vodounists. Possession involves the temporary displacement of the person's *gros-bon-ange*, which could be considered their soul, while the *lwa* takes control of their body. This is, understandably, a difficult process, and the more experienced the Vodounists, the smoother the process will be. It is extremely rare to see uninitiated people or newly-initiated Vodounists being possessed.

While the *lwa* is present at the ceremony, he or she will dance, collect the offerings presented and speak with the followers, particularly those who have a special connection with that particular *lwa*. It is a chance for those people to strengthen their relationship with their *maît-tête*, and for the *lwa* to pass on any information or blessings to the community.

The entire ceremony may continue for hours, depending on the nature of the gifts and the length of the possession. Eventually however, the *lwa* leaves, and the sacrifices and gifts, having been received by the *lwa* and infused with their energy, are eaten or taken by the Vodounists, and the ceremony is officially over.

Some ceremonies, such as those that celebrate particular events or holidays, may vary in structure, but at the core of each is the connection with the *lwa*, and the strengthening of the community.

Contemplation is intense focus with enlightenment as its goal. The act of inner reflection that can help us to see the parts of ourselves that remain in shadow. Contemplation allows one to move forward taking action in the world in which we live, helping to determine our next step along our path and which path to take at each crossroad we encounter.

In order to answer this question I've decided to take and adapt a passage I wrote for my book *The Gospel of Falling Down*. In the book I'd just been talking about the notion that it's often the falling, the breaking, the failures in our lives that (ironically) bring us closer to the deep inner treasure of our true selves. But how, I then ask, do we get to that place without having to fall or crack open? Here's how I answer:

There is hope. There is hope in the form of an ancient spiritual practice that will allow us to visit our inner treasure. I am speaking of the worldwide and multi-religious practice of meditation/contemplation. No matter how important (or busy) a role we have in life, contemplation can help keep us close to who we truly are.

Of course contemplation is simple but not easy. When we meditate we seek to become alert and aware in a way that normal (mind-dominating) life does not encourage. Contemplation is not about going off into a dream state or falling asleep. In fact it's the exact opposite – it's about waking up, waking up from a dream (the dream that is the treadmill of life).

We usually live our lives in the future, wishing for this or that to be different, or in the past, regretting, resenting, and even wishing we were back there. Neither the future nor the past is real. They exist only in our minds as mental projections. Of course the past happened and the future will happen, but we are not in either place NOW. Today we are *here*. Contemplation is about helping us to re-connect with the present moment and live in the NOW, and now is where the gold of our true self exists.

Many people who meditate/contemplate regularly begin to notice that they start living more and more in the present moment, and thus sense a reconnection of mind and body. It is, however, important to realise that meditation is not about a 'goal' to achieve. If anything, meditation helps us to see that the goal is already here. Inside every one of us is a treasure more precious than any chest of gold. It is the *same treasure* that we find through the cracks after our falls. Contemplation helps us to begin to see it again. It pulls back the layers that we have allowed to suffocate our true Selves.

But how do we do it? How do we meditate? How do we quieten the ceaseless flow of thoughts and confusions that buzz incessantly round our minds, and keep us either in the future or the past?

One tradition that can be found in Christianity, Buddhism, Hinduism and many other places is the use of the *mantra*. A mantra is a single word or short phrase that is repeated over and over again during a period of contemplation. It keeps the mind (the little-me) occupied and in a sense stops the inner chatter, helping us to gradually re-awaken the experience of being alive and alert NOW. It can be said verbally but it is usually said inwardly. The important thing is to keep saying the mantra calmly and without any sense of hurry.

What should one use as a mantra? Well it could literally be any word or phrase you choose, even one from a different language to your own. In fact, for me using my own language is likely to conjure up associations or spark off my over active imagination, so I find it better to use one from a different language. Some Christians have found great profit using the Aramaic word 'maranatha' which means 'come lord'. I myself (after beginning a new language course) use a Swahili word, 'Nina-amka', which means 'I awaken'. It really does not matter what the word or phrase is. The important thing is to stick to it. Some Zen practitioners simply count from 'One' to 'Ten' over and over again as their 'mantra'.

The mantra is not magic. It's simply meant to help concentration, so our thoughts begin to slow down and eventually stand still. As I said, contemplation is simple but not easy. Saying the mantra (especially when one first starts) takes a great deal of determination. If you get bored or distracted you must carry on, always re-focussing on the saying of the mantra if your mind wanders, and wander it will! Don't worry about wandering thoughts, and don't worry if it seems like you are getting nowhere. Let me repeat, meditation is not a race, and it's not about getting anywhere, *but being here*. Just keep gently guiding yourself back to the mantra. It will do its own work.

So how do we begin to meditate? Sit comfortably, either in a chair with your back straight and feet firmly on the floor, or on a cushion, with back straight and legs crossed. It's important to be relaxed and comfortable, but alert and attentive. You might like to close your eyes so as to focus inwardly. However I personally find this increases my imaginative thoughts, so I tend to allow my eyes to remain just slightly open so I can half-focus on the ground in front of me. Allow your hands to rest where it feels natural, perhaps with palms open and upward. Begin to take some deep breaths and start to allow yourself to relax. After breathing deeply for a while you can begin to say the mantra. If it has two syllables, like the word 'abba' say 'a' on the in-breath and 'baa' on the out-breath. Four syllable words like Nina-amka also fit to this rhythm, 'nina' on the in-breath and 'amka' on the out-breath. The important thing is to gently allow yourself to say the mantra in some sort of rhythmic way, like a pulse.

When it begins to feel natural you may try watching/following your breath as it enters and leaves your body (still saying the mantra of course). This observation of your breathing can help to develop a real awareness of your body, and of all the sensations and movements of it. You may even begin to feel your actual heart beat, and be aware of the blood flowing around your body as the heart pumps away.

Focus on the saying of the mantra. Don't look for results, fruit will come anyway. Just allow the mantra to do its own work in your life.

1400 years ago in a city on the Arabian Peninsula, a young man went into the desert and climbed into a cave, deep in the side of a mountain. He often did this and enjoyed this time alone to contemplate his life and his community, the days he spent in this solitude refreshed and focused him, returning to his family revived. Many in his community missed him in his absence because he could always be counted on to turn to for help, advice and solutions to community problems. He was affectionately known as the 'Trustworthy'.

One day, while he sat in the cave reflecting on his life and the challenges we all face with family and community, an Angel appeared to him. "Read," the Angel commanded the man. "But I cannot," he replied. "Read in the name of the Lord They God," the Angel commanded again. The man fled from the cave in fear and horror for he believed he was losing his mind. He begged his wife to cover him with a blanket so that he could hide. His wife, a remarkable woman herself, listened to her husband's distress and felt his pain, but eventually she managed to convince him to go back to the cave, for if this apparition was truly sent by God then he had been chosen for a great purpose.

It was his ability for self refection, his engagement in contemplating the punctuations of his life that gave him the strength to return. That day the religion of Islam was revealed and the man became the Last Messenger of God, his name is Mohammed (peace be upon him) and his wife Khadijah was the first person to embrace Islam.

The religion and way of life revealed to this humble man all those centuries ago guides over one billion people all over the world today. Even though they hold the same faith, their cultures are varied and wide and so the practice of this faith can look very different from one culture to another. The common thread that is the same no matter who you are or where you come from is that Islam teaches its followers to hold a deep connection to self reflection and contemplation. It is a religion of self discipline and this cannot be achieved without the ability to recognise ones strengths and weaknesses.

The month of Ramadan (the 9th month of the Islamic calendar) is dedicated to this consciousness. During this month Muslims abstain from all food and drink from sunrise to sunset, but this is not simply about not eating and drinking, its aim is self discipline and self reflection. When you have depleted energy from lack of sustenance your demeanour changes and the resistance you would normally hold towards looking deep within yourself dissolves and you are empowered by the ability to contemplate yourself, your place in the world and your effect on it.

> "[Those] Who remember Allah while standing or sitting or [lying] on their sides and give thought to the creation of the heavens and the earth, [saying], 'Our Lord! You did not create this aimlessly...'"
> Quran 3: 191

One of the guests I invited to an interfaith group I ran was an Anglican Nun.

I remember, when she was asked this very question, her provoking words: "Contemplation is about God. Meditation is about me!" At the time I completely agreed with her, and could see how that defining difference could be of a great help in clearing the mind and attending to one's spiritual musings. But as I journeyed on in my faith, as I became first a pantheist, then more of a panentheist, I realised that such delineation was not something that fit into my own spiritual view-point.

Initially the thought of pantheism, this earth being divine, of divinity being a part of this planet, and divinity being within existence upon the planet, was incredibly attractive. And I could never reject that notion of innate divinity within creation and existence. But I began to ponder the simple question, what if earth didn't exist? If we weren't here, if this pulsing planet, Gaia if you will, was not breathing, would divinity cease? Indeed, does divinity cease once we leave this planet, or, if not, is the divinity existing within another planet in a parallel universe the same as this divinity? I began to reach a conclusion, personally, that while this planet and existence is indeed divine, there is also a larger divinity, beyond, which would exist whether we do or not, but, like dropping a napkin in some water, we are gloriously a part of that larger divinity. This conclusion, that we are within the limitless Divine, but it is also beyond human parameters, informed my view of contemplation. I adopted the very Celtic notion of panentheism.

I have, within my life, a place for prayer, for silence, and for meditation, and I would consider all of these words to be synonymous with each other. I have tried Buddhist meditation, Yogic breathing relaxation, shamanic drumming, transcendental travel and the wonderful Christian Meditation, taking the word MARANATHA, which means 'Come Lord', and using it as a mantra with breathing exercises. I have achieved some amazing results from all of these exercises. Yet, the thing that works the most for me, that allows me to feel that transcendental and communicative relationship with the limitless Divine which I crave, can be summed up in one word; stillness.

It is the action of taking time out, switching off the external stimulus we take for granted, ceasing the din of busy humanity, and just 'being' that allows me to feel true contemplation. And because I am a panentheist, the journey into stillness starts with moving inwards. The neo-Platonists often spoke of the notion of the statue already being within the marble, one just had to cut away the stone to get to it. One has to journey inwards, and find that source of divinity, and then, once there, explode outwards into the mysterious limitless divine beyond. I would be less than honest if I said I achieved this all the time. But, when I have made a concerted effort, I have experienced some wonderful contemplative images, and each and every time I make that effort, I strive to achieve that again.

In Sikhi Meditation or contemplation on the Name of God is Naam Japna or Naam Simran.

Simran in Sikhi signifies meditation. The prime purpose of meditation is to improve the quality of living. This is possible if we regularly become one with our inner spirit/self (Atma) which leads to union with the 'Creator', the 'Source of Being', the 'Source of Existence', more commonly known as Waheguru Parmatma (God). Our Atma (soul) is the seed of Parmatma. Our Atma is like the wave which originates from the ocean, our God. It is the flame which originates from the creator, momentarily takes shape and then recedes back into its source.

Great stress is placed on Naam Simran. A Sikh is required to lead a virtuous, pure and pious life. This virtue can be attained by always remembering and repeating the name of God with full concentration, breath by breath. Naam will create love and affection for all those who are created by God. It is strongly believed that a pious person would be compassionate and contented. He will aspire to serve the needy. He will have no enmity with any one as he knows that God lives in every human being. Hurting of humanity would hurt God. So serve His Creation to serve God and remember the Name of God day and night. The mortal can attain God by living in Him, by dying in Him, by Naming Him and in loving Him

Naam Simran is the only way to attain unity with God. Guru Nanak Dev established God's golden rules for leading a pure and pious life. He preached the concepts by practically enforcing them in his life first.

To most of us, quality of life is primarily what we desire most in this human form. Basically these desires culminate into the following tangible/objective categories: health, wealth and success. We collectively have one desire which is intangible and subjective... HAPPINESS!

The first three are the sum total of all our materialistic desires. Living the Sikh way, as a grahasti (householder/worldly person) requires such aspirations – they are essential ingredients of human life. Sikhi does not advocate renunciation or becoming an ascetic. Sikhs must study/work hard, earn an honest living, be successful, share their earnings with those in need and, at the same time, seek spiritual enlightenment. Sikhs contribute positively to society, and do not become a burden to it.

Happiness, on the other hand, is a very elusive pursuit. True happiness only comes if we develop a degree of contentment (santokh),which comes with spiritual enrichment and the awareness that materialistic achievements are only illusory. We need to develop the ability to achieve worldly success, yet being able to detach ourselves from the end results – this is the key to 'santokh'. We have been given the gift of human form and we are advised by our Guru that this form has been granted to us so that we make an effort to meet our 'Karta Purakh', the creator. (Bhayi prapat manukh dehoria, Gobind Milan ki eh tere beria.)

Therefore, though the basic necessities of living – health, wealth and success – are very important, we must place meeting Waheguru as our prime motive in human life. Our efforts in getting closer to the ultimate aim of meeting Waheguru bring us health, wealth, success and, most importantly, happiness. Happiness can only come with Naam Simran. A great number of successful people are extremely unhappy because they lack spiritual nourishment, and suddenly find an emptiness which just cannot be filled. This emptiness is spiritual thirst. We must do something about this spiritual thirst from the earliest possible moment like right now, if we are not already doing something about it.

All Sikhs are be encouraged to do Simran in a systematic manner as a personal effort.

The Sikh method of Meditation/Simran is called "Naam Japna" – recitation of the name of Waheguru. It is to remember at all times that he is everything to us. Therefore regularly invoking his name and finally becoming one with him. That is ultimate peace. Naam Simran is the activity to draw closer to Him and becoming one with Him.

Naam Japna is as simple as taking time out regularly to sit down and to recite: 'Waheguru, Waheguru, Waheguru...' or 'Satnaam, Satnaam, Satnaam...'

Naam Simran nurtures 'Chardi Kala', confidence, self esteem and everything positive and good. One feels fully protected when one does Naam Simran regularly. Naam Simran helps you to realize your full potential and helps you reach your aspirations in this life. It acts as a 'protective clock' against adverse elements, negative vibes, depression, lack of confidence, and other physical and mental ailments – a protection against evil.

Contemplation or meditation is an important part of daily life for a Celtic Pagan. To understand our place in the world we need to devote time to reflecting on our interaction with the cycles of the night and day governed by the sun, the monthly waxing and waning brought by the moon, and the yearly turning of the seasons dictated by our position in the solar system. Through reflecting on this interaction we come to appreciate the wonders that surround us and of which we are part; we give thanks for the awe-inspiring world we live with; and we are inspired to be the best that we can be in honour of the true magnificence that surrounds us.

As the Wheel of the Year turns through the seasons our spiritual journey is planned. Winter is for deep reflection about what we want to achieve in the coming cycle and how that can be brought about. Spring is the time for spiritual as well as physical spring-cleaning. Now is the time to clear the 'weeds' from our lives – those things that are holding us back and blocking our spiritual growth – and to plant the 'seeds' of what we wish to achieve in the future. It is the time to put into action the reflections of the winter. By summer we should be able to see the 'seeds' growing strongly as our planned changes head to fulfilment. Autumn is the time to harvest the changes that were sown, to give thanks for what we have achieved, and to get ready for the coming time of reflection on where we succeeded, where we failed, and how we can do better in the next cycle.

To plan this spiralling journey effectively we need to be aware of the cycles that surround us and flow through us; to be aware of the intricate and myriad ways in which we are interconnected with all aspects of the natural world; to understand that our place is to work in harmony with the natural cycles rather than trying to control and bend them to our will. By observing the physical world around us and the changes in our surroundings – the altered behaviour of animals, the growth and ripening of fruit and vegetables, the way the landscape changes through the seasons – we can reflect on how the seasonal turnings can alter our perceptions and actions. We begin to understand why we feel sluggish and withdrawn in the cold, long dark nights of winter yet full of joy and life in the warmth of long summer days. By allowing ourselves the stillness to make these observations of the physical world we learn the lesson of living in harmony.

Celtic Pagans also believe that by understanding the natural cycles they can be become aware of the happenings in the co-existing, overlaying 'otherworld' of Spirit. The otherworld is not a separate time and place, it is in the here and now; it is inter-woven with the physical world like a beautiful and complex Celtic knot. The coming together of this complimentary duality of the physical and spiritual makes us complete; without being able to access both facets of our being we are incomplete and therefore out of harmony with the web of life. Our ability to perceive the otherworld also has a natural cycle, with the veil between the worlds being thinnest at Samhain leading into the dark of winter – the time especially suited to deep reflection and planning of the your spiritual journey. As the Wheel of the Year turns, each season is a portal offering the opportunity to increase our understanding of the sacred wisdom inherent in the cycle of life, death and rebirth. It is through experiencing these changing cycles that we can understand and know ourselves and our place in the world and in the web of life. Through the cycles of the years our understanding of ourselves and our place in time and space increases, leading to a greater connectedness with every-thing around us. This is why it is so important to make time for stillness, contemplation and reflection each day.

A recent addition to my own meditative practice has been the use of sacred strands, sometimes called Pagan rosaries or prayer beads. A strand is created by reflecting first on the subject of the meditation and then choosing beads that resonate with each facet of the meditation you are creating. For example, you may begin with 'I honour the ancient Ones, the ancestors, and the wisdom they have passed down the generations'. These strands can contain as few or as many beads as you need, for each strand is unique to its purpose. I have found this an excellent way to focus my mind for meditation.

As well as daily contemplation, meditation is used to prepare ourselves for the rituals associated with the changing seasons, the phases of the moon, and any healing work that we may be involved in. Through this type of meditation we 'ground' ourselves and make our connection with the earth and the spirit otherworld even stronger than usual. This type of meditation begins with focussing the mind and preparing ourselves physically and mentally for the task before us. This may include ritual washing, where the cares and connections to the everyday world are washed away; anointing with specially chosen oils to aid our concentration; preparing the sacred altar with candles of specific colours and flowers of the season; burning incense; chanting, drumming, or by many other means. Daily meditation practice makes it much easier to focus your mind for ritual work.

Ultimately meditation is a means of connecting with the Divine within which links to the transcendent Divine which is the interconnected web of life. It reminds us of our place in the being that is our planet.

Contemplation is conscious reflection on one's Own Holy Self – on the innate, immanent, indwelling divinity that is Self.

When I hear the word 'contemplation' I immediately think of meditation – the art of focus, of cultivating and becoming present within stillness, of flowing within the Chaos and residing within the Cosmos. A Tibetan Buddhist might chant *Om mani padme hum* which translates roughly as "Hail the jewel in the lotus".

Contemplation to a Pagan, and specifically in my experience, translates as conscientious cultivation of consciousness (to employ alliteration). In the WildWood Tradition of Witchcraft we sometimes define Witch as an *individual who is aware, and through ignited awareness seeks to serve and celebrate the Life-Force inherent in Self, Community and Cosmos.* Perhaps the true distinction between a Witch and anyone else (mystic, initiate, devotee or not) is that as Witches we work constantly and consistently to ignite our awareness – to become deeply and intrinsically aware. This is the road to contemplation, and contemplation leads the way.

For many spiritual traditions contemplation concerns the transcendent, perhaps even the moral absolutes (or edicts) embodied (or commanded) by the worshipped deity/divinity. This may have some relevance to those Pagans who work with and reverence specific deities (Gods and Goddesses) and other spirits, beings and aspects/concepts/ideas. However as referred to previously Pagans are rarely moralistic dualists, therefore when we are focussing on adoring a specific deity or spirit we are doing so with the conviction of indwelling consciousness also. While we may simultaneously understand and relate to the being as existing autonomously/independently outside of our own psyches, we also engage on an internal level with all divinity. Therefore much contemplation in Paganism is theological or perhaps more correctly, theurgic (from the Greek *theurgy* – 'the work of the Gods'). Philosophically many of us will often say *"All things are of the Gods"*, therefore we embrace all aspects of Life as lessons in the Great Mystery which is multi-faceted and ever-deep.

Contemplation concerns Infinity and Infinity is boundless. One of the priests of the reclusive Sabaen Order (a mystic group drawing upon several cultures and customs including the West African diaspora) refers to Divinity as infinite and articulates that 'one' (the numerical value) is the farthest one can be from Infinity. To limit the Divine to an objectified value of 'One' (without qualifying this as an adjective of interconnection and wholeness) is to restrict the expression of Life and therefore to negate it. Pagan contemplation starts with 'I do not know' and it ends with 'Now, I do not know'. This isn't as superficial as intel-lectual or even religious ignorance, but is an authentic humility that resonates with the ever-deepening, ever-spiralling convictions of an intelligent Divine presence and power. The gnosis (Greek for 'knowledge) which we attain to in our magickal and philosophical pathways is a temporary thing which shifts to introduce ever-new elements. We are limitless and to say 'I know' is relevant only to a momentary fragment of a vast ocean. To say 'I am' is better.

One definition of 'contemplation' is "concentration on spiritual things as a form of private devotion". Another is "a state of mystical awareness of God's being".[32] These are closely linked to the concept of 'meditation', as "to meditate" is "to engage in contemplation or reflection."[33]

Bahá'u'lláh urged His followers to spend time each day in prayer and meditation:

> "Meditate profoundly, that the secret of things unseen may be revealed unto you, that you may inhale the sweetness of a spiritual and imperishable fragrance..."[34]

Specifically, He encouraged us to reflect each day on our deeds and their worth. Other than this, Bahá'u'lláh did not specify a particular approach to meditation. Instead, each individual is free to choose his or her own meditational form.[35]

Bahá'u'lláh revealed scripture which not only refers to the process of contemplation but provides rich food for that activity. Two passages which I particularly treasure are below.[36]

"O Son of Spirit! I created thee rich, why dost thou bring thyself down to poverty? Noble I made thee, wherewith dost thou abase thyself? Out of the essence of knowledge I gave thee being, why seekest thou enlightenment from anyone besides Me? Out of the clay of love I moulded thee, how dost thou busy thyself with another? **Turn thy sight unto thyself**, that mayest find Me standing within thee, mighty, powerful and self-subsisting."[37]

"O My servants! Could ye apprehend with what wonders of My munificence and bounty I have willed to entrust your souls, ye would, of a truth, rid yourselves of attachment to all created things, and would gain a true knowledge of your own selves — a knowledge which is the same as the comprehension of Mine own Being. Ye would find yourselves independent of all else but Me, and would perceive, **with your inner and outer eye**, and as manifest as the revelation of My effulgent Name, the seas of My loving-kindness and bounty moving within you."[38]

The Bahá'í Faith teaches that meditation and prayer are essential to bring about the state of spiritual communion that unites man with God. This spiritual nourishment then becomes the basis for the development of the individual and society.

"...the core of religious faith is that mystic feeling that unites man with God. This state of spiritual communion can be brought about and maintained by means of meditation and prayer. And this is the reason why Bahá'u'lláh has so much stressed the importance of worship. It is not sufficient for a believer to merely accept and observe the teachings. He should, in addition, cultivate the sense of spirituality, which he can acquire chiefly by the means of prayer. The Bahá'í Faith, like all other Divine religions, is thus fundamentally mystic in character. Its chief goal is the development of the individual and society, through the acquisition of spiritual virtues and powers. It is the soul of man that has first to be fed. And this spiritual nourishment prayer can best provide. Laws and institutions, as viewed by Bahá'u'lláh , can become really effective only when our inner spiritual life has been perfected and transformed. Otherwise religion will degenerate into a mere organisation, and become a dead thing."[39]

Judaism has traditionally been a religion of words, rather than of silent contemplation. We Jews don't do silence particularly well, although meditation services have become increasingly popular in recent years. The rabbis were very concerned that the proper words be said, since they originally conceived of prayer as a direct replacement for sacrifices after the Temple was destroyed. Some prayerbooks even make provisions for when prayers are mistakenly omitted or (more likely) worshippers arrive late. The words were seen as what was important—the silences would take care of themselves. The rabbis actually provided a suggested 'silent prayer' to insert into the service to make sure that even at times of quiet contemplation, the right words would be said!

Our most holy day is Yom Kippur—the Day of Atonement. For a full 24 hours, we stay away from entertainment, from work, even from food. Our hearts are meant to be given over to the process of contrition and repentance. These are by far the longest worship services of the year—even in our Progressive synagogue, we hold eight hours of worship in the twenty-four hours. Not surprisingly, there is little time given over for contemplation—there's just too much to say! On occasion, I will stop the service and invite my congregation to take some time to do their own spiritual work. Some will continue to read and study the prayers, while others are comfortable with the silence.

It is interesting to note that there are so many Jews who have embraced Buddhism that there is even a term for them: Bu-Jews. It is clear that Buddhism—especially Zen Buddhism—may offer something that Judaism lacks. Jews who are seeking out a contemplative experience are sometimes frustrated by our love of words. I myself am no fan of silence, but I seek to create silent spaces for those who feel closest to God when words are absent.

Mindfulness (*smrti*) is commonly seen as a crucial facet of Buddhist meditation. For a Buddhist, this is indeed the motivation, process, and achievement of the path. To be aware of oneself each and every moment, and the moral effects of one's every action: this is true mindfulness and the foundation of a sharp mind that can meditate and develop wisdom. Genuine contemplation therefore cannot be without it. Contemplation involves stilling the mind into a quiet, peaceful state and cultivating the energy (*vīrya*) to concentrate on spiritual matters. Aside from those occasions of sudden epiphanies or revelation (which rarely seems the privilege of the common seeker), it would be difficult to imagine a disciple of any faith tradition who could pray, contemplate the mysteries of sanctity, or sit in solitude with the Divine without a steady and earnest spirit. Contemplation is not daydreaming, nor is it merely hooey, wishful thinking. It is a vigorous mindfulness of the transcendent's love and compassion.

Aside from accepting all the basic techniques of Theravāda meditation[40], Mahāyāna Buddhism has a fully developed framework of devotional contemplation known as *buddhasmA ti*, or mindfulness of the Buddha. This mindfulness is a cornerstone of the Pure Land School, which worships Amitābha, the Buddha of Infinite Light and Life. Amitābha has exerted an immense religious and cultural influence on all schools of Chinese Buddhism and much of East Asia. This school is based on the three Pure Land *sūtras*[41], which tell of a bodhisattva called Dharmākara. He undertook forty-eight vows as part of his ambition to create his own paradise for sentient beings, a Pure Land where there would be no hindrance to learning the Buddha's Dharma. His Eighteenth Vow was the most important: that he would not become a Buddha unless any being could be reborn in his universe by thinking of him with devotion. His vows, according to Chinese Buddhism, were fulfilled long ago, and his paradise: Sukhāvatī, or the Land of Ultimate Bliss, is indeed now open to all beings that think of him with a sincere heart and call on his holy Name.

Mahāyāna Buddhists are encouraged to stay mindful of the Buddha of Infinite Light every waking moment, and especially at the point of death (where one's emotions and thoughts will play a role in one's next rebirth). Contemplation of Amitābha and his infinite compassion is therefore to 'keep in touch' with that most compassionate Reality that is always present.

CHAPTER FIVE

What Happens When We Die?

It is my personal belief that our energy goes back to the planet upon our death, and we are reborn in some form to help our own Spiritual development, and that of the collective consciousness and the Universe as a whole. Because the human condition is as complex as it is, it is my belief that each person determines what happens to them when they die. For those that believe in reincarnation, the cycle continues. For those that believe they go to heaven or hell upon death, that is the afterlife they have created for themselves. For those that believe we simply die and that is it, there is nothing afterwards, that is the afterlife that is created for that belief.

Do you know the saying 'two Jews, three opinions'? Believe it or not, this applies to the question of life after death as well. It is a source of great fascination to those from other faiths that Jews are so unsure what happens to us when we die. After all, this is at the heart of some other religions—particularly Christianity. By contrast, Judaism is a religion of this world, not the next. I often say that I really have no idea what will happen to me after I die, although I do hope that my soul will live on after my body. What I know for sure is that I have today. What will I make of this day, which is a gift from God? Will I squander it on petty quarrels and silly things? Or will I treat it with the reverence it deserves and use it to its full ability?

Judaism does include a number of (mutually contradictory) beliefs about what happens after we die. In one belief, the soul is reunited with God and loses its separate existence entirely. In another school of thought, the soul is elevated to Paradise and spends eternity enjoying a rich spiritual existence. A classical rabbinic belief is the resurrection of the body: according to this school of thought, our souls are suspended after death and then restored to our bodies when the Messiah comes. Yet another belief is that our souls transmigrate into a new body and begin their earthly journey all over again. And yes, there are Jewish atheists who believe that the soul dies with the body. I have personally encountered Jews who hold each of these different beliefs. In many cases they pray together quite happily. After all, we would each hope and pray that the day for our death is quite a distance away!

Death is the one thing in life we can be sure about and that is why religions have beliefs about what it means! Everything else 'might' happen to us: we might get married, be rich, be happy, have children, open our own business or travel the world, but the only real certainty is that we will die.

It is not surprising that people have always asked questions about what, if anything, happens after they die. Ideas about what happens after death, and its connection with how life is lived on earth, are a fundamental part of all religions. The details may differ between religions, but belief in an afterlife almost always helps people to make sense of life (particularly when life seems unfair), gives support and comfort at times of loss and bereavement, and provides a purpose to life.

The ways in which religious people deal with death and the funeral rites they carry out are usually very closely linked with their beliefs about life after death. Funeral rites are very important because they show respect for the dead and, in some religions, include various ceremonies which people believe are necessary to ensure that people go on to whatever their next life will be. Perhaps more importantly, they give the relatives and friends of the deceased time to mourn and show their grief in a certain way. People often say that showing their grief formally helps them to get over their loss.

Sikhs believe that everything that happens is *Hukam* – the will of Waheguru (God) and they should live their lives according to God's will (*Hukam*). Sikhs believe that Birth and Death is the prerogative of the Almighty God-Akall Purkh-the Supreme True Entity, and that one who is born, is bound to die.

Sikhi teaches that people are essentially good; the divine spark within them needs only to be fanned into a flame of goodness. Sikhs believe in the presence of the divine soul within man. Sikhs believe that meditation on the Granth draws them closer to God; it cleanses a person and instills godly qualities in him.

Sikhs cremate their dead. In the Sikh homeland of the Punjab this often happens on the day of death but in other places it may take longer so that relatives can travel to the funeral. Placing the dying person on the ground or making a gift of cows and the deliberate exhibition of grief by beating the breasts and wailing is discouraged. Instead, Sikhs are commended to turn to the Gurur Granth Sahib for solace and guidance. The body, clad in clean clothes, is laid on the pyre and a *granthi* recites the Ardas for the deceased prior to a close relative, generally the eldest son, lighting the funeral pyre. As the body burns the late evening prayer (*Sohila*) is recited. The ashes of the deceased are scattered in running water whenever possible.

In the days following a death, it is customary for the Sikh scriptures to be read aloud in their entirety. Whether this is a continuous 48-hour reading or an intermittent reading will depend upon the wishes of the bereaved family.

As in the world's other religions, the Bahá'í concept of life after death is deeply integrated into teachings about the nature of the soul and the purpose of this earthly life.

The soul does not die; it endures everlastingly. When the human body dies, the soul is freed from ties with the physical body and the surrounding physical world and begins its progress through the spiritual world. Bahá'ís understand the spiritual world to be a timeless and placeless extension of our own universe – and not some physically remote, material or removed place.

The Bahá'í writings explain that after death we will discover mysteries of which we have been unaware in this world and behold the beauty of God. We will remember our life on this earth and realise the distinction between people in respect to soul and conscience.

"As to the question whether the souls will recognise each other in the spiritual world: This is certain; for the Kingdom is the world of vision, where all concealed realities will become disclosed.

...The mysteries of which man is heedless in this earthly world, those will he discover in the heavenly world, and there will he be informed of the secret of truth...

... The difference and distinction will naturally become realised between all men after their departure from this mortal world. But this is not in respect to place, but it is in respect to the soul and conscience. For the Kingdom of God is sanctified from time and place; it is another world and another universe. ...in the divine worlds, the spiritual beloved ones will recognise each other, and will seek union, but a spiritual union. Likewise, a love that one may have entertained for any one will not be forgotten in the world of the Kingdom. Likewise, thou wilt not forget the life that thou hast had in the material world."[43]

Bahá'u'lláh taught that individuals have no existence previous to their life here on earth. Neither is the soul reborn several times in different bodies. He explained, rather, that the soul's evolution is always towards God and away from the material world. A human being spends nine months in the womb in preparation for entry into this physical life. During that nine-month period, the foetus acquires the physical tools (e.g. eyes, limbs, and so forth) necessary for existence in this world. Similarly, this physical world is like a womb for entry into the spiritual world. Our time here is thus a period of preparation during which we are to acquire the spiritual and intellectual tools necessary for life in the next world. Bahá'ís view life as a sort of workshop, where one can develop and perfect those qualities which will be needed in the next life.

In this context, heaven can be seen partly as a state of nearness to God; hell is a state of remoteness from God. Each state follows as a natural consequence of individual efforts, or the lack thereof, to develop spiritually. The key to spiritual progress is to follow the path outlined by the Manifestations of

God.[43]

Bahá'u'lláh wrote:

"Know thou, of a truth, that if the soul of man hath walked in the ways of God, it will, assuredly return and be gathered to the glory of the Beloved. By the righteousness of God! It shall attain a station such as no pen can depict, or tongue can describe."[44]

I was recently asked to give a reflection on All Souls and All Saints Days at the Cafe Church I run as a part of PAX, or Progressive Anglican Christians, which is a part of St Thomas' Anglican Church, Toowong, Brisbane.

I spoke about the festival of Samhain, the festival in the Celtic lands of many of our ancestors. At this time of the year in those lands, heading into the winter, there was death everywhere. Not only the obvious death of vegetation and trees all around, but also the death of many animals, it was the time of slaughter, when people were killing their livestock to prepare for the harsh snowy months ahead. With death everywhere, it makes sense that reflection about death and what was on the other side took place. And the main reflection of Samhain was that, at this time, the veil between this world and the next one was at its thinnest, or even completely gone. It was a time of spirits, a time where you were careful walking on Samhain Eve in case you wandered down the wrong path and entered into the otherworld, where a day would serve as decades in the mortal world! It was a time where loved ones passed through that veil could come home. It was a time of customs like leaving a spare setting at the dinner table or, as I always do, leaving a wee dram of whiskey out for your ancestors to wet their whistle! In short, it was a time when the great mystery of death, of the afterlife, of the divine, ceases to be beyond, and distant, and instead appears before your eyes.

I embrace that concept, that not only at this time of the year, but all year round, our loved ones are not far away, but all around us. Those saints, whether the protestant universal definition or the more Catholic definition, are not in some ethereal realm we can never hope to reach while alive, but rather here and now. To think of us as a part of an eternal, immanent and communicative fellowship, unbound by the spectre of death, where we can ask our loved ones to help, as much as we can ask our best friends on this side of the veil to help, that, to me, is exquisite.

But this does not mean I adhere to the notion of a linear ascent of the soul. As a Christian, at least technically, I am meant to believe that after death we join with Jesus and those passed before us in heaven. But then, as N.T. Wright puts it, there is meant to be a 'life after life after death'. The traditional Christian view-point is that one day there will be a general resurrection, a day when the Kingdom of God is set up on this earth, and we will cease being dead, and be physically and joyously alive once again, but now immortal, in a land where no suffering or death can ever touch us again. I can say, through many discussions with fellow Christians, that most have abandoned the latter part of the above notion, and instead see the after-life as an eternity in heaven within God, whatever that may be. However, I personally reject this concept, as attractive as it is.

I am one of a surprising number of Christians (though many remain shy about admitting it) that includes reincarnation within their Christianity. This is not such a radical notion, there is a strong tradition of reincarnation within Judaism, the wellspring of Christianity, there are passages in the Greek Bible or New Testament that seems to point to the notion, and my adherence and love of Celtic traditions and spirituality mean that the transmigration of the soul is something I had to at least contemplate, at the most embrace, which I have done.

So I see the journey after this life as one passing through that veil, which is all around us, and into the discarnate realm, or summerlands, or heaven, or God. Then I would become one with the Limitless Divine, which I believe would include saying G'day to Jesus, and also become one with that aspect of the soul that never leaves the discarnate realm, and take a soul rest. There would be a time of learning from this life, re-energising, and then coming back to this planet, at some time and place unknown for now. I believe that many of our loved ones will be there with us, maybe in different guises, but there nonetheless. My notions are very similar to Celtic notions of reincarnation, perhaps mixed with general neo-pagan notions of the summerlands etc. And the worth and validity of these notions comes from a simple equation; it completely and utterly feels 'right' within my soul.

And that it is more than good enough for me.

When confronted with the question of the afterlife, I enjoy repeating the cliché that one has no idea because one isn't dead yet. We simply do not *know for complete certainty* what happens when the physical elements dissolve. However, I believe very strongly in a spiritual conception of life after death. Of course, unless the Three Poisons of greed, hatred and delusion are cut away, one is certain to be reborn again and again, with no conscious control over one's future. We could be reborn as gods or animals. The human rebirth is the rarest and most fortunate, because it is in the human state that one is in the position to do spiritual practice.[45] The objective of all Buddhist traditions is to put an end to the kind of rebirth that is caused by ignorance.

I draw inspiration from the vast Mahāyāna *sūtras* that provide answers to the question of the end of life. In East Asia, the most famous eschatology belongs to the Pure Land School. As mentioned above, Amitābha's promise is that any being that calls upon his Name with devotion and sincerity will be reborn in his paradise, Sukhāvatī. I also noted that the time of death is where one's emotions and thoughts play an important role in one's next rebirth. It is therefore crucial to keep one's thoughts happy and forgiving, free of regret, and full of compassion for all beings. One should keep Amitābha's Name in mind constantly (hence the common practice of reciting using prayer beads). With a purified mind and loving thoughts, one will be assured of a good rebirth, but with Amitābha in mind, one will really be taken to his paradise, be it by his entire entourage of bodhisattvas or by a celestial representative.

The details of the Pure Land are manifold and are described beautifully in the three Pure Land *sūtras*. Due to space I can't elaborate here, but it is said that when we arrive we're reborn, cross-legged, in divine lotuses with closed petals. Depending on the gravity of one's bad karma or sins, one's petals might open immediately, or it may take a couple of aeons! But the good news is that all lotuses eventually open, for Amitābha ultimately rejects no one. And there in the Pure Land is only peace, transcendence, and Dharma. It is the final stage of the journey before Buddhahood itself.

Like all other religions, death in Mahāyāna Buddhism is approached with a reverent attitude of faith. It is approached with confidence in the benevolence of the Buddhas and the liberating insights of Buddhist philosophy. Perhaps the most important thing is the reminder that we are all sentient beings that wish for happiness, yet all sentient beings suffer and die. We share each other's existential joy and ultimate fate, and that alone should warrant our care and concern for one another.

According to Theravada Buddhism, when we die our consciousness continues in another body. This is commonly referred to as 'rebirth'. Consciousness can be seen as flowing like a stream. It is not an independent entity like a soul. It is simply a complex network of processes. In the same way water molecules flow together, consciousness acts like a stream that continues after we die. It is important to note, however, that consciousness does not transmigrate in Theravada Buddhism. It does not leave the body and then transplant itself in another body elsewhere. Immediately after the last moment of consciousness in one body there is the first stirring of the next moment of consciousness in a new body. In this way, bodies act like the banks of a river with consciousness flowing through them. There is no break or inter-ceding states between bodies.

Rebirth can occur in any sentient being in the universe, whether it is a human or an animal. In addition, there are many heavens and hells in Theravada Buddhism into which one can be reborn. Our rebirth is determined by our *karma*, the actions we have done in previous lives. These actions have produced habitual tendencies in our consciousness that influence our rebirth. In the same way that a vast, fast flowing river develops banks that are broad and steep, a consciousness of a certain type is sustained by a particular type of existence.

However, the relationship between physical form and previous *karma* is relative. For instance, being reborn within a wealthy family may not necessarily be the result of 'good' actions, since the circumstances of that rebirth may cause great suffering. Likewise, rebirth into an impoverished environment may in fact be conducive to enlightenment and, therefore, be a result of 'good' actions. In this way, our *karmic* tendencies are so complex and relative that we cannot overly generalise about what types of consciousness arise in which types of existence.

If we obtain enlightenment we are no longer subject to our *karma* since we no longer experience the world personally. We have let go of identifying with our egos as 'I' and the objects of our senses as 'mine'. In this way, we are released from the causal effects of our previous actions and we are freed from the process of rebirth. The ignorance that perpetuates the process of rebirth has ended. So what happens to an enlightened person after rebirth has ended? Such a question contradicts the nature of *nirvana* since all concepts of 'person' and 'I' have ceased. Such a conceptualisation runs contrary to the truths of the interdependent and impermanent nature of things. For instance, to say "the Buddha does or does not exist after death" indulges in notions of independence and permanence. If it can be described at all, it is perhaps helpful to consider *nirvana* as being an unconditioned state that is without birth, without death and without suffering.

For me existence is a continuing cyclic spiral of life, death and rebirth. Death is merely another portal through which we pass finding a new life – another link in the chain of existence. Death is a part of life, a part of the natural cycles of existence. As such it needs to be acknowledged and accepted as a stage along our path. It does not need to be feared.

Just as Celtic Pagans have no concept of the oppositional duality of an all-good God and an all-evil Devil, we have no concept of heaven as a distinct place of eternal bliss or hell as an alternate place of eternal punishment; each divorced from the physical world which we now inhabit. We do believe in 'other-worlds', but these worlds are part of the fabric of this world, not separate from it – they overlay the natural world and are contiguous with it. It is possible to journey between these worlds as the physical and spiritual realities are seen as multiple threads in the Celtic knot of existence rather than as distinct and separate worlds.

It is important to understand that time itself is not understood as a linear concept but a cycle. Thus, life is not seen as a straight line with birth at the beginning and death at the end – it continues cycling through time, forever changing. Just as the days, months, seasons and years continually 'die' and are 'reborn' – so it is with us. By observing the natural cycles and working with them, rather than trying to control them, we understand that after death there is rejuvenation and renewal – not oblivion.

For Celtic Pagans what happens in the here and now is what is important in this life – to live the best way you can, be the best person you can in the continuing now. The 'reward' for living a good life is actually the life you live, the people, animals, places you connect with – learn from and share this beautiful world with. This is 'heaven' or 'hell' – depending on our intentions and actions, their consequences and effects. This life and how we choose to live it is not an audition for a place in a better (or worse) future afterlife; this is it. That is why it is so important to appreciate the world we have, to look after this awe-inspiring planet, its environments and its inhabitants – human and non-human, to seek social and economic justice for everyone.

Rebirth is understood differently by different people. For some it is the belief that the soul or consciousness has lived many lives, learning the lessons that are needed to continue life's journey, and will live again to be reborn in human form to continue the journey. This is not seen as a burden as in Buddhist samsara, but as a limitless opportunity to achieve an immense variety of possible learning and experiences. Others see rebirth as the continuing story of life. We learn from the wisdom of the ancestors and from our own experiences and pass this knowledge to the coming generations. In either case death and rebirth are about the story of our journey which is the story of our relationships and interactions with the world around us. As we are all linked through the web of life, our stories reverberate and echo and ripple through all the strands that connect us to everything else. Our stories can be visualized as the chain of life, the river of life flowing through time or the complex Celtic knot of existence, but the essence is the same – we are all joined to every living thing that exists, has existed or will exist.

Emma Restall Orr explains her understanding of what happens after death in her insightful and challenging book *Living with Honour: A Pagan Ethics.* I would like to share her words with you.

"When we die, a part of our song dissolves in the mud of the grave or the dance of the flames; a part continues to be sung by our tribe, by those with whom we've shared love and food, sweat and blood; a part disperses in the wind with our breath, our words, the stories folk will tell of us in years to come; and possibly, if we wish it or cannot let go enough to avoid it, a part of our consciousness will remain coherent enough to coalesce once again into the intention and creativity of another material form, perhaps another human being, maybe even as a descendent of a tribe we have been a member of before." (p141).

What is important is that our consciousness remains connected to everything we have 'touched' in life. As the physical and spiritual bodies are inextricably linked – to each other and to every component of the web of life – our songs and stories continue. Ultimately, what we do during this life is much more important than what happens to our consciousness after death. To live the best life we can, to live with honour, to exhibit courage, generosity and loyalty, to treat all life on this planet as equally important in the vast scheme of things. If we can do this then death will hold no fear and walking through the portal to the next life will be done with a sense of excitement for the adventure that awaits.

As a Pagan I am less concerned with any perceived afterlife than with the apparent, immediate and sacred Here and Now. I do not attempt to placate or please any spirit, deity or force that may judge my 'moral fibre' after my physical body decays, because I believe it is more important to be present in the unfolding and eternal moment, rather than to anticipate a reward or punishment. My ethics are not motivated by either – my Ethics are motivated by the simple idea that to be good is good and not that in doing good I will be rewarded. In this sense I reject the notion of the Threefold Law often conveyed in eclectic variants of modern Wicca.

Briefly the idea of the Threefold Law or Law of Return stipulates that if we do good, good shall return to us three-times enhanced; if we do bad, bad shall be returned to us three-times enhanced. What is being spoken of is not so much a cosmic multiplication of 'cause and effect', but the notion that our actions breed reactions which are intensified in effect. Due to this perceived metaphysical law a Wiccan might casually say that she/he does not do evil because she/he would not want evil returned. This is not Ethics, because conversely, one might say "I do good to have triple-good returned to me" (and I have heard this said many times). I understand the Threefold Law to be a simple observation of action, reaction and consequence – that is all. Again, and ultimately, I attempt to do good because it is good to do so.

All of this may seem completely unrelated to the afterlife or what might happen to us when we die, and that is because I am illustrating the point that as a Pagan it is not of immediate concern to me. However, many Pagans do profess a belief in reincarnation and/or transmigration of the soul as in early animist cultures; perhaps, I am somewhere in between. I do consciously recall many of my past-lives and as someone who does not believe in 'coincidences' there are too many of those to make these past-lives seem fanciful or irrelevant. I generally use the Jungian term 'synchronicity' to refer to this marvellous and mythic interconnection and unfolding of our lives in fated ways.

Pagans will often claim Nature to be their teacher and thus when I look to Nature I see cycles and seasons, ebb and flow, tides and patterns. The fruit of the tree contains its own seed which will perpetuate its continuous rebirth. I tend to think the soul possesses similar seeds which will sow its future fate. Newton observed that all is energy, and that energy cannot be created or destroyed, it can only change and transform, this would also definitely apply to the soul/s (I believe we have three each, as do many cultures and religious/mystical traditions, including Judaism and the Kahuna of Hawaii).

Death is but a door; a renewal of the soul and its revitalisation and transformation into something 'Beyond' (across the Sunless Sea to the Land of Youth as some Witches might say). Perhaps there is a realm of rest as the Wiccans attest to in their belief in Fair Elphame's Land (essentially Faery-Land – the realm of our ancestors and the Beloved Dead) or the Summerlands (also a Spiritualist concept), or even Limbo. I cannot honestly assume or pretend to know and, while I may have had countless private experiences which demonstrate certain realities or truths, I would never wish to become arrogant in my conveyance of them. I am a proponent of infinite possibility and this great wonder-voyage of Life, Death and Rebirth is one that I can without a doubt proclaim I am ecstatic about!

Having been part of a Christian understanding and experience of death and now following the Islamic faith I must be honest and say it has taken me a long time to reconcile the stark differences in the two practices.

As a Christian, my experience of death was one of loss with the funeral being a celebration of the life of the diseased – a place to address the grief of those left behind. A Muslim death centres on the person that has died, with less attention given to those in mourning. This can seem so harsh when comparing the two. When my father died the visits, care and compassion were centred on the family he left behind. His funeral celebrated the impact he had on the world and the legacy he had left behind in his children. So, having had such a personal experience of death as Christian, I struggled with the Islamic view and with what seem to be a cold expectation of those suffering such grief. A Muslim funeral is about the dead, for 40 days people read the Quran and offer prayers for the sake of the deceased. The family is left alone to be supported by very close family and friends in their great grief and encouraged not to engage with the wider community during this time. When I first encountered this I found it heartless – where was the constant stream of visitors to comfort and console? The funeral was just as stark; a simple saying of the specific prayers with no mention of the life left behind and all done with 24 hours of the person's death.

But as with all things that we do not understand, it is only when we allow ourselves to look through the eyes of others instead of expecting them to view their lives through our eyes, that we can have the ability to appreciate both forms.

To put it simply, Muslims spend our lives preparing for our death – and the funeral is for the dead. Everything around this experience is centred on the soul of the one on their journey to God.

Once someone has died we believe that they are met with Angels who will guide them on their journey; until the Day of Judgment we will live in either Paradise of Hell according to the lives we have lead.

On the Day of Judgement (the sixth Article of Faith), all those will be called to account in front of our Creator. Even though the Prophet Mohammed (peace be upon him) is our most beloved Prophet, it will be Jesus who will come to earth and speak for us – plead our case, to put it simply.

"By Him in whose hands my soul rests! It is definitely close in that time that Isa (Jesus), Son of Maryam, descends amongst you as a just ruler."
Ahmad bin Hambal, al-Musnad, vol 2, p. 240

If our initial destination was Hell, on the Day of Judgement we may be resurrected and taken to live with God in Heaven, so even after death Muslims believe our offspring can have an impact on the final destiny of our souls so it is of paramount importance to have lived a full, conscious life with all those around you and to leave a legacy of compassion and love as these deeds will definitely follow us in death.

Death is a natural and inevitable part of life, the moment that gives definition to life. As in many religions, death in Vodou is not the end of one's existence. In Vodou cosmology, there are three parts to each person. The first, the body, is the physical matter, and it is this part which ages and dies. The second part is the *gros-bon-ange* and can, for the sake of simplicity, be considered the 'soul'. It is the repository of each person's knowledge, history, experience and intelligence, and is the metaphysical double of the physical body. It is considered the immortal twin of the physical body, and lives on after death.

The third element of each individual is the spark of higher conscience, the universal commitment towards good, known as the *ti-bon-ange*. It is this part which cannot lie, which guides the *gros-bon-ange* and the physical body towards a life of goodness and honesty,. Ultimately, it is the *gros-bon-ange* which decides whether or not to listen, but the goal of the Vodounist is to allow the *ti-bon-ange* to help develop and enforce a collective morality in each community. The *ti-bon-ange* is not only a personal guardian, but it is what unites all people as spiritual brethren.

At the moment of death, the *ti-bon-ange*, as that part of the individual which is the most anonymous, removes itself from the body, and is thought to hover close by, observing, for a period of nine days, or until the body is buried or cremated, and then returns to heaven to reunite with the greater cosmic divinity.

After the immediate detachment of the *ti-bon-ange*, a

ceremony is conducted to facilitate the removal of the *gros-bon-ange* from the physical body, and the *maît-tête*, or *lwa* who are living 'in the head' of the deceased. There is a strong connection between the *maît-tête* and the *gros-bon-ange*, almost like that of parent and child, and the *gros-bon-ange* must be released from all ties so that it can be free. This ceremony is therefore very important.

Once completed, the *maît-tête lwa* returns to the spiritual waters, the home of all spirits, ready to be called upon again. The *gros-bon-ange* also heads to the spiritual waters, and must remain there for a period of one year and one day, in a period of oblivion which reflects the physical death of the body. After that, there are two possible paths. It may remain in the spiritual realm always; often returning to an element of the realm that most reflects its 'true' home (which for many Vodou practitioners, particularly those of Caribbean heritage, is Africa). Or alternately, the *gros-bon-ange* may be summoned by the living family and community members to return to their realm as a *lwa*. This is most commonly done if the deceased held great knowledge and wisdom that the community does not want to lose. Vodou is a religion with no dogma or text, and therefore lived experience is an extremely valuable asset to the community. Great leaders, *Oungan* and *Manbos* are often reclaimed as *lwa*, and may stand alone, or join the greater *lwa* families with which they identify.

As a non-dogmatic religion that can vary from House to House, Vodou is very welcoming of new ideas and philosophies, and there are only rarely concepts that conflict on a deep level. One Vodounist once described Vodou as a "type of gumbo – you start with a basic recipe, and add your own spices for taste". Some of these new "spices" have shaped the way that some Vodounists view life after death, and concepts such as reincarnation are common, particularly in urban American Houses, where practitioners have been influenced by Buddhism and other Eastern religions.

This is the very hardest question of all answer. In fact, because of that, Adrian had to patiently wait an entire year for me to begin the task. I'm not sure why this is. I don't know what this question does to throw my mind into disarray.

Could it be that my ministry is tied up with death more than anything else which makes it an uncomfortable subject? No, I don't think that's the reason at all. After all, I find the constructing and then the officiating of funerals to be truly satisfying. I have the privilege of helping families of all backgrounds, creeds and perspectives through these deeply painful times and I am always honoured and moved to be used in this way.

Or is it my Christian background and my constant theological journeying that makes the afterlife such a difficult subject? Yes, I suppose this is getting closer to my difficulty. After all, though still a Christian, I am (and have pretty much always been) in conflict with the traditional Judeo-Christian understanding of the afterlife. In a way my term 'afterlife' demonstrates the problem. There really is no 'afterlife' when it comes to the traditional Judeo-Christian perspective. That might come as a shock to some but creedal Christianity does not believe in the 'afterlife' or 'spirit world' or 'cosmic plane' etc., neither does it advocate the 'transmigration of souls' or their 're-incarnation' or being trapped in our world in the form of 'ghosts' etc. Creedal Christianity (and the Judaism that it came from) teaches 'resurrection,' *the resurrection of the BODY.*

Of course, because Christianity was born into a largely Hellenistic world and, soon after its birth, mutated from a wholly

Jewish religion to a largely Greek religion (taking on board the major Greek philosophical schools of thought) it was inevitable that Neo-Platonic and other ideas to do with body and soul/pure spirit and impure matter/perfect reality (above) and it's imperfect reflection (below) etc. became absorbed by Christianity.

But, as my theological college tutors (and a number of the students) kept on insisting, the original Judeo-Christian tradition does not see the body and soul as separate (one, the 'immortal soul', leaving the other at death) but teaches the resurrection of the body as a glorified physical/spiritual body.

However in my experience most people I've ministered to at the time of a loved one's death, Christian and non-Christian alike, do tend to believe in the immortality of the soul and it's transmigration after death, either to a spirit realm or to another body (re-incarnation). Popular novels and movies also generally hold this viewpoint, whether it be the classic 'Ghost' with Patrick Swayze as the dis-incarnate soul trying to tie up loose ends before departing to the white light above, to the modern day fairy tale of Pan's Labyrinth, where the heroine makes her way to a beautiful afterlife after being tested in a gruelling way.

These popular books and movies clearly represent the beliefs of many of the general public, and they can be shocked when they learn that this is not a Christian belief.

And there's my conflict. *I am with the public on this one.*

Endnotes

1   Borg, M.J *The Heart of Christianity: Rediscovering a Life of Faith*, New York: HarperOne, 2003

2   *K oangkar* consisting of the Punjabi numeral *Ek* (one) and *Oangkar*, meaning 'there is one God'.

3   Like previous Messengers of God, Bahá'u'lláh used the masculine pronoun when referring to the Creator. To have done anything else would have violated all conventions of Arabic – the principal language in which Bahá'u'lláh wrote. Bahá'u'lláh stated explicitly, however, that God is beyond any comparison to human form or gender. Accordingly, the issue of whether to refer to God as "He," "She," or "It" does not arise in Bahá'í discussions.

4   Abdu'l-Bahá, *The Promulgation of Universal Peace*, p.173

5   Bahá'u'lláh, *The Kibáb-i-Iqan*, p.142

6   'Abdu'l-Bahá, *Paris Talks*, p.26

7   Bahá'u'lláh, *Gleanings from the Writings of Bahá'u'lláh*, pp.49-40

8   Bahá'u'lláh, *Gleanings from the Writings of Bahá'u'lláh*, pp.105-106

9   'Abdu'l-Bahá, *Some Answered Questions*, p.222

10   Adapted from the website www.bahai.org "The Bahá'í Concept of God"

11   See Guang Xing (2005) for a recent and superb study of the evolution of Buddhology from India to China.

12   The *buddhakṣektra* has two meanings. First, it is the land in which a Buddha works to liberate sentient beings. Secondly, it is a purified realm in which only a Buddha can live. The first definition can be either mundane and defiled or pure, whereas the second can only be celestial and pure (Guang Xing, 2005, p.171)

13   The central Buddha of this text is Vairocana, who is identical to Śākyamuni (Śākyamuni's *sambhogakāya*) (ibid. 170)

14 A term coined by feminists to encourage the perspective and inclusion of the Divine Feminine. Pagans embrace all gender/s and non-gender/s.

15 Faith also denotes perseverance in the bodhisattva path, which is conventionally held to require three aeons (more than 300 billion years per aeon) of training! Faith in Mahāyāna Buddhism is anything but a simple escape from the world.

16 Skorupski's translation (2002), pp.20 – 1

17 'Abdu'l-Bahá, *Some Answered Questions*, p.6

18 'Abdu'l-Bahá, *Star of the West Vol 24*, p.350

19 Bahá'u'lláh, *Tablets of Bahá'u'lláh*, p.156

20 Bahá'u'lláh, *Gleanings from the Writings of Bahá'u'lláh*, CXVIII

21 Bahá'u'lláh, *Bahá'í Prayers, Long Obligatory Prayer*, p.15

22 Pilgrim's note of a conversation with Shoghi Effendi, *Principles of Bahá'í Administration* – a compilation prepared by the National Spiritual Assembly of the Bahá'ís of the British Isles 1950, pp90-91

23 'Abdu'l-Bahá, *Selections from the Writings of 'Abdu'l-Bahá*, p.178

24 'Abdu'l-Bahá, *An Early Pilgrimage*, p.40

25 John Esslemont, *Bahá'u'lláh and the New Era*, pp.195-196

26 'Abdu'l-Bahá, *Some Answered Questions*, pp.250-251

27 'Abdu'l-Bahá, *Paris Talks*, p.177

28 `Abdu'l-Bahá, *Some Answered Questions*, pp.214-215

29 Adapted from website www.bahai.org "On Good and Evil"

30 Gethin, 1998, p.71

31 Fox, M. *A Spirituality Named Compassion*, Minnesota, MN: Winston, 1979, p34

32 *Webster's 9th New Collegiate Dictionary*, Copyright 1983, p.283

33 Ibid, p.738

34 Bahá'u'lláh, *The Kitab-i-iqan*, p.8

35 Adapted from the website www.bahai.org "Prayer, Meditation and Fasting"

36   Note that the underlined and bold words in the quotes below have been highlighted by the author for emphasis in the context of the question under reply, and are not part of the original text.

37   Bahá'u'lláh *The Hidden Words, Arabic No 13*

38   Bahá'u'lláh, *Gleanings from the Writings of Bahá'u'lláh,* pp.326-327

39   From a Letter written on behalf of Shoghi Effendi, published in *Bahá'í News* 102 (August 1936), p.3

40   These include *śamatha* (breathing)" and "*vipaśyanā* (concentration)", the Four Divine Abodes (*brahma-vihāra*), and many more. It must be remembered that the concept of enlightenment in Mahāyāna is different to Theravāda (Theravādins aim for the NirvāAa of the saint whilst Mahāyāna stresses the possibility of Buddhahood itself). Each tradition's path of practice has therefore diverged, especially in regard to meditative practices since it is through meditation that one attains enlightenment.

41   These are the larger and smaller *Sukhāvatīvyūha* and the *Amitāurdhyāna sūtras*. The former two were composed in India, whilst the last may have been completed in either Central Asia or China (Gethin, 1998, pp.263 – 4). There are other *sūtras* that speak of other Pure Lands presided over by other Buddhas, but their influence has not been able to match that of Amitābha's.

42   'Abdu'l-Bahá, *Tablets of 'Abdu'l-Bahá Vol 1,* pp.205-206

43   Adapted from the website www.bahai.org "Life, Death and the Soul" and "Heaven and Hell; a Bahá'í View of the Afterlife".

44   Bahá'u'lláh, *Gleanings from the Writings of Bahá'u'lláh,* p.161

45   While Buddhism is commonly known not to anthropomorphize the universe for the sake of a human purpose, the human state is no doubt the best one can be born into.

CHRISTIAN
ALTERNATIVE

Throughout the two thousand years of Christian tradition there have been, and still are, groups and individuals that exist in the margins and upon the edge of faith. But in Christianity's contrapuntal history it has often been these outcasts and pioneers that have forged contemporary orthodoxy out of former radicalism as belief evolves to engage with and encompass the ever-changing social and scientific realities. Real faith lies not in the comfortable certainties of the Orthodox, but somewhere in a half-glimpsed hinterland on the dirt track to Emmaus, where the Death of God meets the Resurrection, where the supernatural Christ meets the historical Jesus, and where the revolution liberates both the oppressed and the oppressors.

Welcome to Christian Alternative... a space at the edge where the light shines through.